UNB

UNBROKEN

The Woman
who Walked Again

Georgina Hurst
with Becky Bond

Scratching Shed Publishing Ltd

First published by Scratching Shed Publishing Ltd in 2021

Registered in England & Wales No. 6588772.

Registered office:

47 Street Lane, Leeds, West Yorkshire. LS8 1AP

www.scratchingshedpublishing.co.uk

ISBN 978-1838489946

Cover photography: Simon Hooley The Image Cella

A catalogue record for this book is available
from the British Library.

Typeset in Warnock Pro Semi Bold and Palatino

Printed and bound in the United Kingdom by

Trecerus Industrial Estate, Padstow,
Cornwall PL28 8RW

www.tjbooks.co.uk

I want this book to prove to you that life changing does not mean life ending. You just have to approach things differently, adapt and overcome.

Life is what you make it. Impossible is only a word.

Much love,
George
X

Contents

Acknowledgements

•

There are lots of wonderful people who ought to be thanked for bringing this book to life, far too many in fact to mention here. I do hope they know that my gratitude is sincere.

I am particularly grateful to my parents and brother, though, whose belief in me has been unconditional.

When I had the idea to tell my story, I knew I wouldn't have the ability to put it down on paper myself. It was purely by chance, then, that an old friend mentioned I needn't shelve the idea because she would be my ghostwriter.

Becky Bond, you gave me the motivation, inspiration and means to get it done. You have helped to tell my story with sensitivity and humour and I'll be forever in your debt.

August 31
•
Dead Day

FOR THE LAST twenty-three years I've celebrated Dead Day; the day *he* – my former fiancé – put me in a wheelchair and inadvertently turned my life around.

It was August Bank Holiday Monday, 1998, and a blast of rare West Yorkshire sunshine had been working its magic over the tightly-packed beer garden in our village; the world and his wife soaking up rays and booze on a bonus day off.

Everyone was in a good mood.

I can still picture a bunch of bawdy women, sandals abandoned, three Lambrinis down, cackling about their latest escapades and conquests. Popped-up parents were stalling home-time with extra packets of crisps for the children, and even the regular old men in the corner had taken their coats off and broken out in smiles.

I felt so happy, basking in my boyfriend's attention after coming home for the weekend from Liverpool, where I worked as a paramedic. I was 24, tanned, fit, and feeling confident in my size ten blue shorts and loose white T-shirt, dark hair recently cut into a bob.

He was 23, his usual jeans and trainers as faded as his blond hair, whch had lightened over the summer and flopped curtains-style over his aqua blue eyes.

As we squashed in together with his friends around a picnic table, I was enjoying feeling his lean body nudging against my diminutive frame, catching the odd whiff of his Lynx deodorant. It was good to be back.

I can see now, though, that I wasn't the focus of his attention that day. His best friends always took precedence and if I wanted to see him, I could tag along.

There was nothing wrong with his pals as such, they were just typical small-town boys really (one a bit podgy, dark hair, questionable teeth, the other lanky, ginger, pale). Not offensive, but no great shakes. At the time, they probably thought they were better looking and funnier than they were, a pack mentality keeping them safe from anything as scary as original thought or new horizons.

But I was happy to be among them. I still fancied my man rotten and loved that other girls obviously thought he was a catch. He knew it too, though. His cheeky smile wasn't just reserved for me, but conjured up at the slightest hint of a fluttered eyelash across the bar.

But he was with me now, and it had been two weeks since I'd seen him, so I was looking forward to the possibility of some time alone together later that night.

We weren't drunk – I'd had a couple of halves of Fosters and, because he was driving for once, he'd had about the same.

It was late afternoon and we were hungry, so supped up and decided to head to McDonald's, the likelihood of ordering a burger from the heaving bar seeming slim. His sidekicks got in one car and I had the luxury of having him to myself in his metallic green VW Golf. The radio switched on with the engine, but it was a special programme to mark a year since the death of Princess Diana.

I wasn't in the mood for doom and gloom, so pushed in my favourite Warren G CD, *Regulate*.

As he eased out of the car park, I wound down my window to let in some cool air and checked behind, to see if the others were following.

They were busy laughing at something, fastening their seatbelts, revving noisily, causing some of the elderly patrons to roll their eyes and mutter.

The route we took is what's known locally as 'over the tops'; a smaller road to Keighley town centre avoiding the boroughs of Bingley and Crossflatts. It follows the outskirts of St Ives Estate – a five hundred and fifty-acre country park with a golf course, stables, fishing lake and huge playground, mostly hidden behind traditional dry-stone walling and oak trees.

As a child I often had picnics there with my Brownie pack (I was a sixer no less) and couldn't count the number of times mum and dad pushed my younger brother James and me on its swings.

Further up, sheep can often be seen grazing beside the occasional Shetland pony, where set-back farms earn extra pin money selling eggs or logs at their gates.

From the brow of the hill, a stunning view of the Aire Valley spills out, showcasing a mixture of traditional terraced housing, high street shops and modern industry nestled among the varied communities living there.

We'd been in the car for about three minutes and I was chattering away about possible wedding venues and who we'd invite to our reception. I didn't notice the Fiesta in front of us driving particularly slowly, but *he* obviously did. 'If that bloody burgundy car doesn't get a shift on, we'll die of starvation here,' he growled.

I took no notice though. It was hot, it was the weekend and I wasn't going to let his temper sour the day.

Then his friends suddenly pulled out, screeching past us and the car in front, one of them laughing and doing the 'wanker' sign out of the window. He was the knob, I thought.

It was an unnecessary risk, the potential damage of which I'd already witnessed in my job. But my man wouldn't be beaten. He was high on sunshine and wanted to race and I just knew he was going to follow.

From where I was sat in the passenger seat, it was hard to tell if the road ahead was clear, but I knew that route like the back of my hand and warned him that we weren't far off a steep hill.

I could tell he wasn't paying attention to me, though, and began to feel very scared, my heart thumping as I urged him to be cautious. But he wasn't listening.

He was smiling, checking his wing mirror to see how soon he could pull out. All he could focus on was catching up with his mates.

I felt my body lurch to the right as he swerved out and then put his foot to the floor. The last thing I said to him – in my old voice – was: 'Please, slow down.'

He broke my neck and leg, shattered my pelvis, tore my liver, my kidneys, my bladder, punctured both my lungs and made me bleed internally.

I was resuscitated twice at the scene, in a coma for weeks, in hospital for months, then rehab for a year. I had to learn to speak again and even now, at times I sound like I'm sloshed.

We'd had a collision at an estimated combined total of 120mph. The 56-year-old lady in the Vauxhall Nova he smashed into suffered a broken sternum and arm. She was doing no more than 40mph. *He* got a bruised leg and a six-month jail sentence.

And when I came around, I forgave him.

It took me twenty years to get the stage where I could live independently again. I've worked so hard to regain my mobility and strength by setting myself crazy goals.

I'll never have the body I had before the crash – I still need crutches or a wheelchair – but the life I've got is better.

This is my story of recovery, the reason why I embrace Dead Day. *Unbroken* is far from being a misery memoir.

I've learned to laugh at some of the ridiculous situations I have ended up in, during my journey since from medically deceased to mobile.

From travelling alone around the world and meeting a one-armed bandit, to cycling across Europe when I suffered chafing so badly that I wished I'd been left paralysed from the waist down.

I've scaled ten-foot walls, walked across hot coals and even endured a Brazilian wax in a carpet shop, all in the name of not letting this thing beat me.

Oh, and I've learned to pole dance.

1

•

Angie Head Holder

HE WAS A huge part of my life for a while. I thought we were going to get married, the whole shebang, but he means nothing to me now.

In proportional terms, he shared about seven per cent of my life. What he did, I will live with forever, and so will he. But we will live with it separately.

He might have ruined part of my twenties, but he won't influence my future and will certainly never be able to take away the safe and happy childhood that mum and dad worked so hard to provide for their children.

It's only now, though, that I'm beginning to wonder whether another incident I was subjected to, aged just fourteen, may have inadvertently led me into his arms in the first place. But one trauma at a time, eh?

I do know that if mum and dad hadn't provided such a stable home life, my younger brother wouldn't have been able to hold it together as well as he did following the car crash. It's because of James that dad could support mum and, in turn, they could both help me in what was nothing short of a complete nightmare.

And James was the main point of contact for the woman who essentially saved my life on the road that day; someone we now fondly call Angie Headholder.

Angie had been driving the burgundy Fiesta in front of our VW Golf. She was with her two sisters, Anne and Josie, their seventy-five-year-old mum and Angie's one-year old baby, Alisha. The five of them were on their way back to their mum's house on Oakworth Road in Keighley after a successful shopping trip to the Grattan catalogue discount store, Manorgrove, in Bradford.

The car boot was piled with bargains, which they were looking forward to spreading out on the kitchen table and poring over again, a ritual they did every couple of months or so and really enjoyed together.

Even though it was a baking hot day, all the windows in Angie's car were up because her mum couldn't bear a draft, always worrying she'd get cold, then proper poorly.

While Angie and her sisters were clad in a mixture of leggings and loose tops, flip flops and hair tied back with matching scrunchies, their mum kept her coat zipped up, handbag held as close to her lap as the Elnett hairspray was to her neat, short perm.

The mood was noisy but jovial inside the car, no music but general bonhomie about the bank holiday. Talk of a possible barbecue at a friend's house, wondering if they'd bought enough booze, if anyone was taking a potato salad, and would Alisha (who was conked out in her car seat at the time) be happy for a few hours if they stayed in the shade?

As all the chatter was going on, Angie kept an eye on

the rear-view mirror, clocking her baby's warm, filmy face in the corner of her eye, thinking how lucky her little girl was to be surrounded by all these women who loved her.

As Harden Road receded behind her mother's and Josie's heads, Angie saw that a car seemed to be approaching dangerously fast. A few seconds later, she checked her mirror again and all hell broke loose.

'Carnage,' they said. 'Utter carnage.'

The next day, an officer from West Yorkshire Police arrived at Angie's house, to take statements from herself and Anne.

Angie invited him in through the back door straight into the kitchen, where Anne was sat at the table, picking at a raffia mat, on top of which sat a half-empty glass fruit bowl with two overripe bananas and a wrinkly apple, tempting a tiny cluster of fruit flies.

'I'm sorry you had to witness what you did yesterday,' the policeman began. 'I can't imagine how awful it must have been. I hope you're both bearing up under the circumstances. My name is Mick by the way.'

He held out his hand to shake. Angie did and Anne half-smiled at him. They thought he seemed right enough.

'Hopefully the scumbag responsible for this will get what he deserves in the end,' Mick said. 'Not that it will be any consolation for the poor lass in intensive care right now – but we'll do our best.'

Mick slipped his jacket off and hung it on the back of one of the wooden chairs tucked under the table, then placed his cap beside the fruit bowl, nodding at Anne as he did so. Angie busied herself filling the kettle with her still-shaky hands.

'It's really important, hard as it may be, to just tell me exactly what you saw,' Mick continued. 'Not what you think you saw or assumed you must have seen. It's very easy for our mind to fill in the gaps if we're not a hundred per cent, so we can take a much time as you need.'

Angie and Anne nodded slowly that they understood. 'Tea or coffee?' Angie asked.

'Tea please. One sugar, thanks,' replied Mick.

Neither of the sisters or their mum had slept much the night before. Everything kept churning around.

Each time Angie felt herself drifting off, new images from the scene of the accident sabotaged any chance of peaceful slumber. There was still so much to process.

The tan which had caught her face earlier that summer seemed to have faded with her hopes of rest and the dark circles under her red eyes told Mick this was going to be a tough statement to take, particularly as he couldn't even console them with news of me being alive.

He knew the doctors were doing all they could, but was waiting for an update. He'd seen some accidents in his time but, in all honesty, with this one he didn't feel hopeful.

Angie shook a few chocolate digestives on to a side plate and, picking up her own cup of tea, gestured for Anne and Mick to collect theirs and follow her into the lounge.

The faded orange curtains were still half drawn from shading the television earlier. They'd been trying to catch the local news to see if there were any updates on the crash, but nothing as yet. They'd get a *Telegraph & Argus* later.

Mick waited for the women to sit down on the sofa together. Then, plonking his tea on top of a copy of the *Radio Times* upon a nest of tables, he positioned himself in the armchair nearest the window.

He preferred it when the seating arrangements weren't so 'job interview', but it was their home and they could sit where they liked.

Mick took out his notebook and pen and cleared his throat. 'So, shall we just start at the beginning and see where we go from there? There's no rush ladies. As I said, take your time,' he formally started, in what he hoped was his best calming voice.

Anne looked at Angie and nodded for her to begin.

'Well, me and Anne were in the car with my mum, my baby daughter Alisha and our other sister, Josie. I was driving, Anne was the front passenger and the others were in the back, with Alisha in her baby seat.'

Angie looked at her sister for reassurance.

She part-smiled, encouraging her to continue.

'We'd all been shopping and were in a right good mood, driving back to my mum's over the tops, just coming up to the back entrance to St Ives. Then these lunatics came racing past us on the bend. They came out of nowhere. There were two cars. One with two lads in it and then the one behind, which caused the crash. I was so angry. My baby was in the car. I still feel sick thinking about it.

'They overtook us just before you get to St Ives, at high speed, on the bend virtually – that really bad one. They nearly ran us off the road and I was fuming.

'We were all effing and jeffing with my mum in the car, and my mum's Catholic, so you don't swear in front of her. And I'm screaming: "I don't care mother, they're going to cause an accident driving like that. Or they'll bloody kill us."'

Anne cut in: 'How Angie kept us on the road I've no idea... But we got around the next corner and we were gobsmacked. It was awful.

'We didn't see the crash happen, it must have been about maybe ten seconds after they'd passed us, further up the road. About 200-300 yards. The carnage just seemed to come into vision in a kind of slow-motion.

'They were driving so fast it took us longer to get to that point. And this lad was running towards us while we were trying to get out of our car. He was shouting at us saying: "George is dead, George is dead."

'And I screamed: "And YOU'VE killed her." I was absolutely ripping. I shouted: "You've nearly killed us and now you've probably killed her."'

Mick was scribbling this down as fast as he could, looking at each woman in turn as they shared the events as they'd experienced them.

'It was awful,' Angie said. 'All you could smell was burnt tyres and petrol.'

Anne then explained that she'd managed to get herself over to the car to look inside. She said she could see I'd been pushed so far over that my passenger seat was in the driver's one, but my legs were still in the passenger footwell. Like I'd been crushed thin. And my mouth was bubbling.

'It was terrible,' Anne whispered, her voice cracking, eyes beginning to glisten as she tilted her head to the ceiling trying to prevent the tears tipping out.

'She was foaming at the mouth and her teeth were bared. She looked all teeth. I really thought she was dying.'

Angie's eyes widened then searched the middle distance, settling on a framed photograph of Alisha just above the TV. Remembering the scene so vividly, her hands cradled her cup of tea for warmth as the full horror came flooding back.

Anne swallowed and continued: 'Then there was this other, older lady in another car. I mean, I'm only a care assistant, but I've had lots of training so think I must have gone into autopilot. I said: "Angie, get in this car with the young lass," but she shouted back: "I'm not getting in the car it's going to blow up." I told her: "It's not, get in here quick and hold her head. I think she's still alive. If she starts fitting or anything, hold her head."'

Angie's eyes re-focussed on Mick as she picked up where Anne had left off: 'I really don't know how I did it. I don't know how I managed to get in the back seat. I had to crawl over somehow because the car was all crumpled and glass was everywhere, pressing into my knees. And I honestly thought it was going to blow up. It was so frightening.

'Then my mother was coming over to help, with Alisha balanced on her hip, so I just shouted at mum to get herself and my baby away. I was so scared the car was going to blow up, I told her to say a prayer.'

Anne then outlined that her and Josie rushed over to check how the lady who'd been in the oncoming car was. She was conscious, but very dazed, and when they looked down they realised her legs were in a bad way too.

As they began talking to her, trying to comfort her, Josie thought she could smell alcohol and wondered if the woman had been drink-driving. But as she looked around the rest of the car, she noticed a bag of groceries with two smashed wine bottles inside. It had obviously happened due to the impact.

Anne said she instructed Josie to just keep talking to the older lady and hold her hand, then she called for one of the lads who'd been in the other car involved to unzip his tracksuit top and pass it over.

'I can't give you this,' he'd said. 'It's new.'

Anne just screamed: 'Give me your fucking top,' then whipped it off him and covered the older lady up. Anne was going backwards and forwards between her, Angie, me and the boys, one of whom by that point had disappeared to the nearest farm to call an ambulance.

Mick shook his head in disbelief. He knew the boys

would have been in shock but not to offer your jacket in a situation like that was something else, beyond a lack of obvious chivalry.

The first of the emergency services to arrive at the scene were the police, or rather, one policeman.

Anne continued: 'I thought, "Oh good, he's come to take over." But oh no, he was like "It's alright, you're doing a good job, I'll go and sort the traffic out." He just left us to deal with it. He wanted to get the driver who caused it breathalysed before any more time passed. I mean, that was one thing. He might have been a dickhead, but at least he wasn't over the limit.'

Angie shifted on the sofa, putting her feet straight out on the pouffe to look at her knees. They were grazed and sore. Not deep cuts, but roughed-up and not yet scabbed over.

'I was knelt in all this glass, trying to talk to the young woman who was called George. I couldn't believe it. And there was an awful smell coming from her. It was putrid. Horrible. I was leaning right over her. It was like acid. Like emptying stomach. I thought: "She's definitely dying. She'll never make it."'

Angie said she just kept talking to me. She can't remember what she was saying, and I obviously can't, because I was almost dead.

It didn't matter what. She just kept thinking she might be the last person to speak to me, so wanted to say something profound, but all that came out was: 'You're going to be alright.' It all seemed a bit trite to her at that moment.

Mick was concerned for Angie and Anne, and suggested they took a break from the statement for a moment, but Anne wanted to keep going.

'I've seen loads of people die, with my job,' she continued. 'And there is a certain smell. She smelled like death. She was obviously deeply, deeply unconscious. There was no blood on her though. None at all.'

What struck both sisters was the lack of co-ordination between the emergency services. They felt none of the professionals really knew what they were doing.

They were looking to Anne for guidance. It was her who told the ambulance team on their arrival that the first thing I needed was a drip. Then it was her who held the drip-bag to get the fluids in me, but she's unsure what they were – saline, morphine?

Brushing her left knee gently with her fingers, Angie continued: 'So Anne was the drip stand and I was holding Georgina's head, hoping and praying that someone was going to take over any minute. The fire crew arrived next and they were no better, just scratching their heads.

'Then, eventually – I can't believe this – but they were going to pull her out from the side of the car door before Anne told them they needed to cut the roof off and get her out on a board.'

Anne leaned towards Mick and looked directly at him. 'So the ambulance guy goes and gets a neck brace and puts it on her, then looks at me and asks: "Is that alright?" I just stared back at him in disbelief and said: "Yes."

'Honestly, that is the truth. I was shocked. There was no organisation or anything. Nobody seemed to know what they were doing. Why did I have to tell them what to do? I'm not a bloody paramedic or a fireman or a policeman.'

Mick agreed that it sounded like a complete shambles, but he had to keep a professional distance. He hadn't been there though he felt that if he had, he'd have had a much better handle on the situation right from the start.

But all he could do was write down what they were telling him. He wanted to keep them focussed on the actual events, not what they thought about the people trying to deal with the aftermath.

Apparently, I arrested a few times. My heart actually stopped while they were working on me at the scene; first of all when I was still on the road, on the stretcher, then in the ambulance as well. I'd stopped breathing.

Moving her feet back onto the floor in the lounge, Angie slumped forward, running her hand across her face.

'When the ambulance drove off to A&E – I presume it was to Airedale hospital?' she queried, Mick confirming that with a nod. 'We were just left, sat there, thinking holy crap, what have we just witnessed? What have we been involved in?'

Anne rested her tea on the arm of the sofa, agreeing. 'We were all in a state of shock. Why the hell didn't people take over? Professionals that are used to seeing crashes?

'Honestly, it's lucky we were there because if we hadn't been, that girl would have been pronounced dead at the scene, I'm sure.'

Angie added: 'And in all of this, the driver who did it was just running around like a headless chicken saying, "I've killed George, I've killed George."'

Taking that statement was a moment Mick says he'll never forget. The way the sisters described the acidic smell coming from me was like he'd witnessed it himself.

The three of them sat reflecting in Angie's front room, all needing a moment when he'd finished writing his notes up. The rest of Mick's tea had gone cold and no one had touched the digestives.

The women didn't receive any psychological support, no counselling to help them come to terms with what they'd witnessed.

They just had to get on with it. But they are more in awe

now of my mum and dad and how they coped. Angie reckons if it had been her own daughter in the crash, she'd have had a nervous breakdown long since.

Angie still remembers the long telephone calls she had with my brother, James, in the months that followed.

They talked for ages as he updated her on my progress and she filled him in on what they were up to, just everyday stuff, for a welcome dose of normality.

Both say it really helped having someone on the end of the line who knew and understood what the other needed at that point in time.

But Angie didn't realise until much later that the guy who had caused it all had actually been friends with James before the crash.

2

•

Double Whammy

THERE IS NO denying that the accident wouldn't have happened if *he* had been driving at the correct speed and not taken such a stupid risk. But once all the facts were gathered, it was concluded that this was the sequence of events:

1 – His friends overtook us, Angie and her family on a bend then pulled back in, in front of Angie's car.
2 – He then overtook Angie and his mates, as we neared the brow of a hill.
3 – As he was pulling back in, another car was coming out of a small track on the left-hand side.
4 – He tried to swerve to avoid the car pulling out, but hadn't seen the on-coming car approaching over the brow.
5 – When that vehicle came into vision, he slammed on his brakes and skidded sideways.

6 – He avoided the car pulling out of the side road,
   but hit the one driven by the 56-year-old woman.
7 – I took the impact on the left-hand side of his car.

And there you have it. The whole incident can't have taken more than ninety seconds. Fortunately, I don't remember a thing because at that point I was dying.

In the local newspaper that week, the paramedics and fire crew were heaped with praise. No mention of Angie, Anne or Josie and all they'd done to help. The sisters thought that was pretty rubbish and, frankly, so do I.

The next thing I heard was mum's voice, six weeks later, on Ward 24 of St James's Hospital in Leeds. She was reading *The Horse Whisperer* to me. It's by Nicholas Evans and was on the bestseller list at the time.

It's about a girl who was hit by a 40-ton truck while out riding on her horse. Imagine? Only my mum could pick something like that. It does have a happy ending, but still.

When I came around it must have been very gradual. I've no recollection of suddenly thinking 'Christ, where am I? What's happened?'

I just remember feeling calm, listening to mum's voice, her Liverpudlian lilt still prominent from where she grew up, only slightly diluted by the occasional Yorkshire-ism.

I'd obviously been in a coma and on a shedload of sedatives and painkillers. It's a miracle my whole family weren't on narcotics too, because the chaos that ensued straight after the accident continued apace. The nightmare *he* had dragged us all into had only just begun.

At some point in the ambulance on the way to A&E, I must have temporarily regained consciousness because when the paramedics wheeled me into Airedale hospital I was screaming about my back.

Then, not long after, I saw *him* and my dad arguing and I was shouting at them to stop. That was the last time anyone heard my voice as it used to be.

Dad was all over the place mentally – and beyond furious. Apoplectic. Even though it hadn't been confirmed that *he* caused the accident at that stage, dad knew.

Then my brother arrived, panic-stricken, running towards the lady in triage, yelling: 'Where's my sister? Where is she?' But she had no time to answer.

As she checked her notes, James shrieked: 'Georgina Hurst? She's been in a car accident.' He didn't wait for the reply, just followed the signposts directing him to the emergency rooms, careering from bay to bay, yanking curtains back, desperate to find me.

The harsh strip lights and beeping machines mixed with the stench of vomit and disinfectant, added to his rising nausea. Then blood drained from his face as he saw me. He was left rooted to the spot, waiting for his brain to catch up and compute the scene in front of him.

Eight people were working on me at the same time, trying to save my life and then stabilise me as best they could. It's technical and brutal but essential, just like a fancier version of plumbing with more blood. I was heavily sedated by then, as the team tried to assess the damage.

They set to business with more drips, infusions and a catheter. At this point they didn't know what was broken and what wasn't, where I was bleeding internally and whether or not I'd survive.

You have to be a certain type of nurse or doctor to want that kind of stress in your life. As a former paramedic, I get that. Nobody wants anybody to die, but the adrenalin is instantaneous when you get that crash call. Suddenly, everything you've learned, all your experience and knowledge, is called upon and brought into sharp focus, enabling you to do all that's humanly possible to save the life in front of you. It's a drug in itself.

But as skilled as the team were at Airedale hospital, they simply didn't have the facilities to cope with the scale of my injuries and decided to rush me to the trauma unit at St James's hospital in Leeds, or Jimmy's as everyone knows it.

I was loaded into an ambulance with heart and blood pressure monitors, my face covered with an oxygen mask. Mum, a doctor and a paramedic joined me in the back. The blue lights and sirens wailed into action for our twenty-five mile journey.

Dad says that once the staff at Airedale realised I was 'one of them' – a paramedic – they let the team at Jimmy's know, who then pulled out all the stops and brought in consultants straight away.

As I said earlier, it was a bank holiday and, as we all know with the NHS being on its knees, it's probably best if you are poorly on a normal Monday to Friday when there's more chance of someone being around who is not a junior doctor or hungover. But nonetheless, they brought in the big guns and I'll be eternally grateful.

That journey to Leeds nearly finished me off. What happened next honestly beggar's belief.

We were blue-lighting it along the A65 in Kirkstall – a busy trunk road, edged by a mixture of shops and take-aways, businesses, a leisure park, cinema and the old Yorkshire Television studios – the type of road that's always choc-a-bloc in rush hour as it leads straight to the city centre, as well as connecting to the main motorways.

Most vehicles were moving out of the way, melting to

the roadside or slowing down for us to pass safely. But some guy in a car, who must have been deaf as a post or just plain ignorant, pulled out right in front of us, so our ambulance driver had to slam on the brakes to avoid colliding into him.

Worse still, the gurney I was laid on in the back hadn't been locked down securely, so as his foot hit the floor, me and the trolley flew into the front of the unit, causing me to smash my head on the partition between the driver and us, further displacing my neck in the process. Unbelievable. Two accidents in the space of two hours. Someone was on a mission to do me in that day.

Mum was in orbit as the blood pressure machine signalled things were not good at all. The doctor leaned over and tried to switch the sound off, hoping mum hadn't clocked it yet, but she was too savvy for them.

'Don't you be switching that off for my benefit. You keep that on,' she said – there never was any arguing with mum. If I'd been conscious and capable, I'd have turned it back on myself just to avoid her wrath.

For some reason, and maybe again perhaps it was because it was a bank holiday, our ambulance journey from Airedale to Jimmy's wasn't accompanied by police outriders.

Usually, in a situation like that, they are a given. They drive ahead on motorbikes, sort of leapfrogging each other to clear the route to make it faster and smoother. If the ambulance had had an escort from Airedale to Jimmy's, we could have had a clear run and arrived in twelve minutes. On Google Maps, that journey suggests you need fifty-two.

I've often been asked if I'd ever thought of pursuing some form of extra compensation for that incident, but I don't want to. What's done is done. OK, the brakes should have been on the gurney, but they weren't.

The guy shouldn't have pulled in front of us, but he

did. If there had been police outriders, the ambulance wouldn't have encountered the guy pulling out. Yada yada... You could be turning that over in your mind for ever. But I seriously doubt any of it was done intentionally.

It was just a culmination of random events. I'm alive, that's what matters. I just hope lessons were learned.

Ironically, driving the ambulance was one of the jobs I loved as a paramedic. I was a Class One driver having had specialist training. I can still handle a car well now – but I had to learn again from scratch and it's not quite as easy as just hopping in and setting off anymore.

There's the slight issue of where I'll put my crutches and the constant annoyance of non-disabled drivers stealing the designated car parking spaces; and getting my wheelchair out of the boot can sometimes be a bit of a bugger.

The ambulance driving lessons were brilliant, particularly going on the skid pads where you have to do a certain amount of manoeuvres to prove you can handle the vehicle.

Hurling it left and right in rainy conditions really teaches you how to drive properly – and safely. Shame *he* hadn't had any of those lessons. I enjoyed the 'narrated drive' part of the training too.

It's basically when someone else is in the car with you and you have to say what you're doing and why. For example, if you're going to overtake a car, you have to tell them: 'Putting the indicator on. Checking my mirror. Pulling out. Passing car on left. This is my speed. Pass the car. Indicating in. Pulling in. Reducing speed.' etc.

If you're decelerating, you have to say what speed you are breaking at. I just loved that feeling of knowing I was fully in control.

I must admit, it's quite a thrill when the lights and

sirens are on and drivers move out of your way. You can see the whole road clearing ahead, like God parting the seas.

When I see emergency vehicles now, I usually don't bat an eyelid. But a few bank holidays ago, when it would have been my 21st Dead Day, I was driving to mum and dad's on a road close to where my crash had been in Long Lee.

Ambulances were screaming past, sirens, the works, and I just burst into tears. I thought, that would have been me they were rushing to save all those years ago. It really caught me off guard for some reason.

But on top of that, I couldn't help thinking that if *he* hadn't driven so bloody thoughtlessly, I could have been the one driving that ambulance to help someone else. It made me miss my old job. I drove a bit further up the road and pulled into layby to gather myself together.

When I arrived at mum and dad's house, I told them what had just happened and how I'd had to stop for a while. But they just said: 'Why?' And I replied: 'Well, erm, it's twenty-one years ago today.' But they just shrugged it off.

If they don't want to talk about it, that's fine, but it's a big thing to me. I don't want them to think I'm being selfish, dragging it all up again – and I could have misunderstood them, maybe. Sometimes I don't understand them at all.

But when I left their house, I did sort myself out again. I slapped my head with my hands and gave myself a good talking to. I just said to myself 'get on with it', because I can't change it.

There's no point thinking 'what if'. I felt a bit better after that. A good cry helps. It does.

3

•

One Per Cent Chance

I WAS IN THE trauma department at St James's for about four hours before I went in for the first major operation. It had taken them all that time to stabilise me.

Mum, dad, my brother and *him* had been told to wait in the relative's room, but dad made it quite clear that *he* wasn't welcome, asking: 'At what point did she tell you to slow down?' He couldn't answer, just took himself out of the room and sat on the other side of the door, sobbing.

James needed to get away from the stifling atmosphere to try and sort his head out, so left to find the bathroom to splash some water on his face.

The slow walk around the corner afforded our James a bit of time to think and check his surroundings. Was he still in Airedale, or at Leeds now? Was it day or night? He was nowhere near a window, so had no idea.

He checked his watch, but couldn't focus on what the

digital numbers meant. Pausing, he leant his lean, five-foot five frame against a wall and looked to the ceiling, saying a silent prayer that I'd pull through. He couldn't have chosen a worse place. And his timing was also dreadful.

Nearby was a curtain, behind which stood one of my surgeons, Mr Matthews, on the telephone to a colleague. They were discussing me. James didn't want to hear, he needed to keep walking and pretend that everything was alright, but he was drawn in, desperate for any nugget of hope. A hint of something positive that he could cling to. He pressed his head back and forced himself to listen.

Mr Matthews was conveying the severity of the vast range of my injuries. In hushed but businesslike tones, he listed all that he knew so far.

The surgeon talked about catastrophic neck injuries, the possibility of paralysis, incontinence, internal wounds which may or may not still be bleeding and severe brain damage, the chances of me pulling through in percentage terms.

It was in single figures. Or rather one single figure. One per cent, tops. 'Basically, she's not going to make it,' he said.

James nearly vomited on the spot. His insides knotted, head reeling as his right hand covered his eyes, then slowly traversed down towards the soft skin between his high cheekbones and jaw, where he pressed the flesh with his forefinger and thumb, doubled over.

Shaking his head, he tried to comprehend what he was hearing, desperately not wanting to believe a word. One per cent, tops. That's all he could think. One per cent, if that.

'Basically, she's not going to make it.'

Just then, the curtain drew back and Mr Matthews emerged, spotting my brother. He realised, judging by the state of him, that he must have heard everything. 'I'm so sorry,' he said and invited James in to sit down.

In gentler terms, he went over the enormous challenges I was facing again; he was calm and sympathetic, but honest.

He gave James the space to ask any questions, but Mr Matthews didn't have any answers James wanted to hear. They walked to the bathroom, where the surgeon left him at the sink, running the cold tap, staring at the mirror.

Now James knew more than mum and dad. Should he tell them? Could he? I was dying. Cupping his hands he scooped the chilled water over his face, hoping the shock of it would bring him out of this nightmare.

He wanted to rewind to that morning when he was happily waxing his new little black BMW in the sunshine, his girlfriend looking on, stroking her pregnant belly. He was going to be a dad. His sister was meant to be an auntie.

It was impossible that this was happening. Impossible that he had more information than his parents. The thought of telling them, also impossible.

Dragging a blue paper towel from the dispenser, he slowly began to pat his face dry, small pieces of tissue sticking to his chin. He noted his eyes were bloodshot but not from crying, from constant rubbing in disbelief.

James took a deep breath and made an effort to tidy himself up, tucking his T-shirt into his jeans and smoothing down his short floppy dark hair, messed up from raking his fingers through it with stress.

He turned to the mirror and made the decision to keep the news to himself. If it was true, they'd find out sooner rather than later. He could barely comprehend it himself, so he knew he wouldn't be able to articulate it to mum and dad.

It took James a long time – years in fact – before he finally sought help in the form of psychotherapy, to allow him to process what had happened. He hadn't realised that the way he'd been dealing with events in his own life following the crash were intrinsically linked to what he'd experienced. My brother was very angry about everything. Road rage was a major issue, but that wasn't the half of it.

I was offered counselling when I was in rehabilitation, but after a few sessions thought 'what's the point?'. All they seemed to want to talk about was *him* – and how I felt about what *he'd* done, and how *he* was going to cope with it.

That annoyed me. I didn't want to talk about *him*. *He* was alright. No broken neck or wheelchair for *him*, just a bruise. I sacked it off.

But some of my friends recently urged me to try therapy again and, after a lot of initial resistance, I found myself on the phone to James, asking him to book me an appointment with the lady who had helped him.

James went one step further and drove me to my first appointment. I wouldn't say I was nervous, just concerned that she might think I was wasting her time.

On the way, he told me I could talk about anything and absolutely none of it would leave the four walls of the Well Being Clinic unless the therapist thought I was in danger of harming myself or anyone else. We parked up and I grabbed my crutches, letting James lead the way. We were buzzed through to the main entrance and in the absence of a lift, slowly headed up two flights of stairs.

The waiting room was at the end of a long corridor, decorated in muted modern tones to make you feel relaxed.

You know the type of thing – a couple of sofas, a water cooler, some plants and a table with high-end mags like *Yorkshire Living* and *Homes & Antiques* dotted about. There were a few abstract prints on the wall for good measure, probably to take your mind off the fact that you're about to bare your soul to a perfect stranger.

When Catherine invited me into her office, I knew I was going to like her. She made us both a cup of tea and we sat on opposite sofas with a table between us.

I told her basic details about the crash and that other incident when I was fourteen. She said she'd never met anyone so matter of fact. We kind of came to the conclusion that before the crash I didn't love myself, and we needed to look at why.

She told me how inspirational she thinks I am, but said I am no good at taking a compliment – which is true, to a degree. I feel uncomfortable when people say nice things to my face.

It's not that I don't want people to think I'm a good person, it's just that compliments are a bit weird. But I felt really at ease with Catherine and after our initial meeting booked a second appointment, just to talk. Just to see.

4

•

Long Way to Go

BY THE TIME my brother had gathered himself together in the gents at Jimmy's and begun the heavy walk back to the relatives' room, Mr Matthews had been in to see my mum and dad.

He'd explained the situation I was facing and let them know that James was already in the picture. The surgeon asked again if anyone had any questions.

There were too many to verbalise. Mum couldn't think about the ninety-nine per cent likelihood of me not pulling through. She focussed on that one per cent.

To her, one per cent was still a chance and she was clinging on to that with everything she had.

When James returned, Mr Matthews said it would be wise for everyone to see me and perhaps say a few words, just in case. He didn't say 'last goodbyes,' but they all knew that was what he meant. I can't even think for a minute what that must have been like for them. Where do you start? What do you say?

Are there actually any words that would in any way comfort a deeply unconscious patient? But an act like that is as much for the survivors as the injured, one last window to say how you feel, apologise maybe, make amends, tell them how much you love them.

As a rule, we're not a slushy family, but an event like that tends to sharpen the senses somewhat. And it was time.

I'd been assessed in the trauma unit and they needed to move fast. I don't know if they all came in together or separately, nor what they said, but I do know that dad didn't think my fiancé deserved the chance of a few final words.

Everyone was suffering. The weight of guilt even *he* was carrying must have been unbearable. I doubt anything could have made him feel worse than he already did.

But anyway, while they took turns to hold my hand, searching for any semblance of a sentence that might offer hope, I lay there, static and unaware.

I was now being kept alive by technology, awaiting the next stage. Some people who've been medically dead, or dying, like me, say they experienced a kind of floating-out-of-their body moment, almost like they were hovering above themselves, looking down on the scene of panic below, but I had nothing like that. I was out for the count.

I wish I had, it would be quite weird to experience your own temporary demise.

Others say they have this feeling of travelling through a dark tunnel towards a light and they're being welcomed by friends and family.

That would have been lovely, but there was no tunnel for me and no bugger waiting at the end of it. Next time, I'm hoping for a whole roomful, like a surprise party.

I wonder if they serve my favourite, pink champagne, up there? That would certainly take the edge off having just snuffed it. But I've no plans to shuffle off planet earth just yet. It's taken me twenty-odd years to get back on my feet and the adventure has only just begun.

After everyone had had their moment with me, I was taken to the operating theatre and the first job for Mr Matthews was to stabilise my shattered pelvis and leg fracture with external fixators. Fixators are basically bits of medical scaffolding, bolted to the outside of your body, held together by screws into your bones.

I had a complex pelvic fracture, classified as an LC 3 (i.e. in smithereens) and a left tibial fracture with compartment syndrome, which is when pressure within the muscles builds to dangerous levels and causes it to swell. It can restrict blood flow, which in turn stops oxygen and nourishment from reaching nerve and muscle cells.

My leg looked like a balloon and they had to cut it open to release the pressure. It left me with a huge scar, which I make no attempt to hide.

I knew about these types of injuries from my paramedic training but, faced with them myself, I developed an acute interest in the real detail once I was well enough. Mainly because I had stuff all else to do during my recovery.

Then the surgeon did something called a laparotomy, which is a big incision into your abdominal wall, so they can get to your abdominal cavity to properly assess the damage.

But get this – the first laparotomy ever performed was in 1809, without an anaesthetic, by a bloke called Ephraim McDowell, a physician from Kentucky. I'm very glad medicine had moved on a bit before it was my turn. I think it would've taken more than a whiff of smelling salts to bring me round after that.

Since 2012 though, trauma units have been better organised and massively improved. Now, a case like mine would go straight to a major trauma centre instead of A&E.

They can control shock better, have cleverer equipment and the added bonus of years more experience.

If I'd had my accident in this decade, it's likely I wouldn't have suffered as many complications during recovery. It would still have been touch and go, but I guess that's why they call medicine a 'practice' – they have to practice on whoever they can until they hopefully get it right. I'm just hugely relieved that coronavirus hadn't surfaced at that time or this could have been a very short book.

My surgery took hours and hours. They did as much as they could, but had to take it one injury at a time. There was such a catalogue of damage that they hadn't even realised my neck was broken until days later.

All my loved ones could do was wait. Every time a nurse or doctor walked past the relative's room my dad would jump up, hoping for a progress report, only to be told, 'nothing yet'. Mum tried to convince herself that no news was good news. James remained silent.

When Mr Matthews emerged from theatre at nearly three o'clock in the morning, he went straight to my family. He was exhausted, but didn't want to hand the job of delivering my outcome to someone else.

Dad really appreciated the respect he'd shown with that gesture. He pulled up a chair and found the words. I was nowhere near out of the woods, he'd said.

There were so many elements which either alone or together, could still mean I wouldn't recover – mentally or physically. It was literally a case of time.

And there were many more operations which needed to be done if I was suitably recovered from this first one. Brain damage was still highly likely.

Mum only heard positives. I'd already lived longer than they'd predicted, so she believed I had the will to survive. She wouldn't hear of anything else.

There was a lot of hugging going on. Not relief exactly, but a glimmer of hope shone between them because I'd made it through the first round.

As the surgeon prepared to leave, mum, dad and James gathered up their belongings and made a move towards the door and ICU, desperate to see me again. But Mr Matthews asked them to slow down, reiterating the need for extreme caution in terms of getting their hopes up. He also wanted to prepare them for what I was going to look like.

I was unrecognisable, my whole body swollen, my face to the point where none of my features were discernible. Numerous drips and cannulas were coming out of my arms and hands. Lines were attached to my heart.

It looked like Meccano was covering the whole of my midriff. The ventilator tube down my throat protruded, the sound of air being pushed in and out of my lungs competing with the beep-beep-beeping noise of the heart monitor.

A catheter drain subtly snaked its way out of the white sheets to an opaque bag in a metal frame at the side of the bed. I was deathly still.

No amount of warning could have prepared them. Less than twenty-four hours ago mum had been pottering about the kitchen in her knee-length summer skirt and little blouse, flip-flopping to the garden for an occasional Silk Cut, a batch of jam tarts in the oven.

Dad had been attending to some paperwork in his home office in the basement, where it was cooler. He still hadn't mastered the art of leisurewear, so was in his regular standard slacks and smart shirt over his midlife middle, his only concession to dressing down being a bit of stubble.

It had been business as usual for the Hursts on August Bank Holiday Monday, until they were plunged into a living nightmare.

Mum didn't see their house again for at least six weeks, choosing instead to stay in a relatives' bedroom in the hospital, with dad. My fiancé also stayed at St James's, but not for nearly as long.

Mr Matthews was due to go on holiday the following day, and the lead orthopaedic trauma surgeon, Mr Malcolm Smith, was returning from his. So after a detailed handover, I was now in new, but very safe, hands for all my future operations. Most unusually for surgeon-patient relationships, my family remain friends with Mr Smith.

Dad even helped to clear his garage a few years later when he moved to America to become chief orthopaedic trauma surgeon at Massachusetts General Hospital in Boston.

After surgery, I was mainly looked after by a lovely nurse called Lou on the Intensive Care Unit (ICU). We're still in touch now. Bizarrely, she ended up decorating my house. Turns out she was doing an interior design course on the side. At the time though, Lou's thoughts were a million miles away from soft furnishings.

Her primary concern was my head injuries. But she says she knew within days of me being admitted to her ward that I'd pull through. She claims to have a sixth sense about which patients will and says it's all to do with the inner fight.

Lou believes that some people, for whatever reason, choose not to. But clearly, I was never going to be that person.

Mum, dad and James were surrounded by close family who'd rushed to get to the hospital in those first couple of days. Mum's sister Pat acted as the main point of contact for extended family members, filtering down news as things progressed, fielding unnecessary visitors.

Mum and dad's best friends, Glynnis and Stephen, were a huge presence when words failed – it was comfort enough just for them to be there.

Although it was *The Horse Whisperer* I remember mum reading when I regained consciousness, she'd filled large parts of time in my initial weeks in ICU ploughing through three other novels at my bedside.

She'd done two Bill Brysons and *Bridget Jones's Diary*, praying that just the sound of her voice might spark some form of recognition in me.

Apparently, mum really got into the swearing parts of the Bridget Jones one. I can imagine her releasing a lot of tension there – especially as every time she looked up from the page she was faced with me in 'rag order', as James would say.

But no matter how much mum read to me or how tenderly dad held my hand or wholeheartedly James tried to channel all his strength and energy into me, I showed no outward signs of improvement for weeks.

It must have been devastating. My friends by this point had set up an informal rota for visits, which was a comfort to my parents. It just gave them a bit of breathing space and the chance for someone else to do the talking for a while.

Mum particularly liked having my friends there because it made her feel like I was still in the land of the living. Like they were still going to be part of my future, however that was going to pan out.

She'd always had a strong connection with my friend Alycia – probably because like mum, she was a teacher. Or maybe because, also like mum, she's your typical glass-half-full girl, with a giggle usually bubbling away behind her pretty, freckly face, framed by a shock of white-blonde hair.

She's the kind of mate everyone should have at least one of. The full package of sporty but not showy, funny but not crass, and never says no to a trip to the pub.

Alycia had mum in stitches in ICU at one point. It's usually so quiet in there, with just the whirr of life-support machines and muted chatter from the nurses, so when Alycia clocked the kidney and urology guy walking past, she left it a few beats, looked at mum then started yelling at me: 'George. GEORGE. Bloody well open your eyes. Look at the guy who's checking your genitals for functionality. He's gorgeous. Come ON George, have a butchers. If he was anywhere near MY reproductive organs I'd never let him go.'

They were killing themselves laughing, mum and Alycia. I wish I could have been a fly on the wall. It's that sort of humour you need to get through something so desperate.

God knows if the urologist heard. I must have seen him once I'd come out of my coma, I suppose, but honestly can't remember him. I think it's fair to say though, that even if he'd been Brad Pitt's twin brother, I wasn't really in any position to be flirting.

In between everyone's visits in the first week, numerous tests were carried out on my brain. It was a tricky issue because there'd been no damage to my skull – no fracture at all. I'd had something called a contrecoup – a fancy word which means your brain gets knocked forwards and then backwards inside your skull, ending up bruised and swollen. It's apparently very common in road traffic or fast impact accidents.

My neck hadn't been as lucky as my skull though, and Mr Smith soon identified where it was broken and scheduled more emergency surgery.

Unbroken

I was then fitted with a contraption called a halo to hold my head and neck absolutely still to give it chance to heal. The metal ring of the 'halo' was attached around the top of my head and held in position by screws drilled into my skull (one of which was particularly difficult to get in and caused problems during removal).

Four metal rods were attached to the ring around my head, which led down to a special, solid bodywarmer with the appearance of a bulletproof vest. There, the rods were held firmly by blocks. It was like being trussed up in graphite. Thank God I was still in an induced coma at that point.

Induced comas are done with intravenous drugs, so my arms must have looked like an addict's by the end of ICU, with all the drips and potions they were pouring into me.

It was the most drugs I'd ever had, having never been tempted by the recreational kind, unlike *him*. It was just weed that *he* was into, with his friends, but I always felt left out because I never wanted any.

I couldn't see the point in turning myself into a zombie, but I never tried to stop him. As if he would have listened.

One of the things we used to do before the crash was drive up to a caravan at the back of an old mill. I say 'we', that obviously included his friends because we never, ever had a date on our own. But often on a Friday night after last orders in Bingley, muggins here, as designated driver, would pile everyone into my car and head to the mobile home, where they'd all do a bong.

They thought they were hilarious, but most of the time were just zonked out. *He* would always inhale too much then throw a 'whitey' and have to vomit outside. Then I'd drive them all home.

Honestly, what was I thinking? What on earth was the attraction? How did I believe *he* loved me?

He obviously knew the consequences of what could happen if I'd been caught with them. I would have lost my dream paramedic job for being used by *him* and his trailer trash friends.

The pupil reaction test was a very regular occurrence on ICU. It's like in the films where you see a nurse with a little torch, lifting up the patient's eyelid to check for a response.

If neither pupil reacts, you are basically dead. If one pupil reacts, that's not so great, but at least you're still here. But if both pupils react, that's very good news.

Fortunately, both my eyes were responding, so that was a massive boost for mum and dad. Mum really felt I was still in there somewhere, that I was listening and understanding (on some level at least) what was going on. She kept busy with anything to pass the time in hospital.

My feet had kind of splayed out on the bed. It was like my ankles were together but the tops of my feet had drifted apart, so with more hope than anyone else in the hospital that I'd walk again, mum attempted to keep my feet as supple as possible.

The routine involved putting these big boot things on me every three hours to hold them together, then taking them off for three hours to let them rest. It might have helped to a certain extent.

James hated seeing the nurses replace the gel patches over my eyelids. They were there to keep my eyes moist to prevent ulceration because I was in no fit state to close them or blink independently. But he felt they made me look dead already.

It was very traumatic for him because, as well as being faced with the horror of me, he'd suddenly had to step up at work, taking over the family business so dad could support mum in the hospital. It was like a slow, pressure cooker effect.

Unbroken

He felt he had nowhere to turn and no time to unburden his tangled thoughts. His girlfriend was due to give birth any day, so he didn't want to give her and the baby any more stress.

Mum and dad were permanently at the hospital so James felt he couldn't collapse in front of them, didn't want to be petty by saying 'I'm upset' when their other child was fighting her life.

And because James's circle still included *him* at that point, he couldn't talk openly with his friends either.

My brother was boomeranging from hospital, to worry at work, to home and back again, in a loop. He didn't have a single minute of downtime in which to process what was actually going on and so began to cultivate quite the attitude to cover up his feelings.

No surprise then that road rage became his thing.

That time alone in his car, driving from place to place, was the only chance James had to think – and woe betide anyone who disrupted that one sliver of silence he had.

Aged 22, his life was not panning out how he'd hoped.

5
•
An Empty Bay

WHILE THE PRESSURE in James's head increased, the swelling in my brain slowly began to reduce and the medical team decided it was time to try and bring me out of my induced coma.

It was a bit of a palaver by all accounts. The doctor dictates when to reduce the drugs and over how long a period of time, but it's the nurses who actually do it. If it doesn't work, the doctor has to be called back to increase the drugs again.

They tried a couple of times by gradually taking me off the sedation, then monitoring my behaviour closely, but I wasn't behaving as I should, so they had to put me back under. The process is called weaning because essentially, they're weaning you off drugs – opiates for pain relief and, in my case, paralysing agents due to the nature of my smashed pelvis, broken neck and leg.

You can't be thrashing about or suddenly reaching to scratch your bum if half your body's being held together by metalwork.

Mum and dad really struggled when the first attempt to bring me back into the real world failed. That's because, like most relatives rooting for their loved ones, when the doctor says: 'We are going to try and bring them out of a coma,' they don't hear the 'try' part, just the bit about being brought around.

It looked like I was having a seizure, which after being still for so long, must have come as quite a shock. It's a really hairy time as drips can be dislodged and all sorts. They wanted to hold my hand, but Lou had to ask them to stand back.

Managing parents can sometimes be harder than dealing with patients because they constantly question what you're doing and why. They need regular reassurance that their child is getting the best care possible. With a ventilated, comatose patient in ICU, a nurse does observations, checks, ensures infusions are working, sores are as good as they can be etc... like a checklist. For days, nothing can change and it's devastating for a family to watch, so a big part of the nurse's job is managing expectations.

Even though I was far, far from better, when I did finally emerge from the coma, it was a very emotional moment for mum and dad.

Mum still insists she didn't cry. The only thing which temporarily undid her, was four weeks after that first surgery when I suddenly developed a very dangerous temperature. It spiked to 42 degrees. You're not meant to live at that heat, but if you do, the risk of permanent brain injury is extremely high.

Usually, when someone has a soaring temperature, it's

because their body is fighting an infection. But on ICU, there are other more worrying factors to take into consideration.

If you've had a serious bang on the head, like I had, then suddenly, nothing works properly. Your 'centres' are all over the shop.

The bit at the base of the brain, which controls things like temperature and pupil reactions, goes haywire. It's your brain's way of saying 'I'm not happy.' And the only way to reduce the temperature is to give more drugs, fluids, via an infusion, the medical term for which is a mannitol.

The medical team decided it would be better if I was put into a side room, just off from the ward, away from any other possible germs, but mum played merry hell.

She'd seen patients be taken into that side room and not come out alive, so was utterly panic stricken. It took Lou and the doctors a lot of persuading to convince her that this move didn't signal my exiting the hospital in a zipped-up bag.

But one doctor, whom we consequently called Dr Doom, told mum that if I survived this then I would end up being a vegetable. And that was when she lost it.

Mum had been just about holding it together until then, but she couldn't bear to hear that. She's never been one for showing her emotions in public, though, and knew she'd have to find a place to let it all out.

She sought out the hospital chapel and, making her way there calmly and collectively, opened the door, let it close gently behind her, knelt at the altar and wept. She looked up and said: 'God, don't let her be a vegetable, take her.'

James had spent another day at the office, fighting fire with fire. As much as he was grateful for the orders flowing in, each one came with a customer asking about my progress. And although he was touched that so many people were offering sympathy and reassurance, it was very draining explaining what stage I was at, every single time. It was heart-breaking for him to have to constantly repeat: 'No change, still no communication.' He tried to separate what was actually happening from his own feelings. Keep it simple. Autopilot. Get the work done so dad could support mum at my bedside. He found himself being short with clients who were only trying to be kind. Then felt guilty for flying off the handle. It was exhausting.

When James finally locked up at work that evening, he made a quick phone call to his partner. He wouldn't be going straight home because mum had rung to say my temperature was through the roof. He needed to see me even though he knew his partner needed him too. More guilt.

He got into his car, clicked the seatbelt on, double checked it, checked all his mirrors then indicated to pull out of the car park, accidentally switching on the windscreen wipers instead. It was cold but not wet, surprising for the end of September, and the scraping noise of the wipers rubbing across the dry screen went right through him.

He couldn't catch his breath as his mind created images of my crash in his head. If it had rained on that bank holiday, I might not have gone to the pub, he reasoned.

I might not have been with *him* in the car. Or *he* might not have overtaken Angie if the road had been slick with water. *He* might have thought twice and then I wouldn't still be fighting for life, one month on. James was furious, even with the weather.

But he swallowed his anger. No time for that. Slapping the wipers off and the indicator on, he edged out and joined the crawling rush hour traffic into Leeds. Now it was the traffic's fault – why was there so much of it? What was the hold up? Shouldn't people be allowed to do shifts to keep things flowing?

My little brother's mind was constantly whirring for solutions, subconsciously searching for coping tools to make everything better.

By the time he arrived at Jimmy's, of course, the car park was heaving. Like him, most people didn't have the luxury of visiting their loved ones in daylight hours so the queue just to get in was at least five cars deep.

James could see the digital sign for the amount of spaces left going down as those in front took a ticket and moved in. Four spaces left and no cars exiting. Agitated, he wound down his window and craned his neck to see if he could spot any other vehicles on their way down the multi-storey.

There was one.

He could see them slowly driving into vision, the passenger scrabbling around for the ticket, no doubt dropped in the footwell after putting her purse back in her dis-organised bag.

He couldn't see past his own situation. Didn't have any more capacity to cope with other people's problems. No thought that the other people in this car park might also be unfocussed, coping with their own catastrophes. He just wanted them to get out of the way so he could get in and see me. They'd had their time, he reasoned, now it was his. Fair's fair. But nothing was fair anymore.

Eventually, enough cars left the car park and yanking the ticket out of the machine, James stop-started all the way to the roof, looking for a space.

He'd seen one, then no. It was a mini, tucked right in. Then an elderly man was reversing out of a spot, so he waited – but he was just straightening up. Why has nobody taken that space yet? Oh, it's marked as a disabled bay.

He considered swinging into it but caught himself

wondering about me. Would I ever be able to drive again? Would I need a blue badge? A blue badge, for Christ's sake. They were for pensioners and cripples, not my sister, he thought. Not for women in their twenties whose job it was to save other people's lives.

Finally, he reversed in between two cars and switched his engine off. Squeezing out of the driver's side he noted the location and headed for the lift.

By this point, he felt the whole world was conspiring against him, resigned to the fact that, of course, the lift would take ages to arrive and then stop at every floor on the way down.

Visitors filtered in and out of the sliding doors. *Please stand clear of the closing doors.* Fingers hovering over which button to press for the correct ward.

James made a mental note to slow himself down from jogging to walking along the corridors. Breathe. I was only around the corner. The place seemed so familiar to him now, he had no need for directions, could tell just by the type of posters on the walls that he was on the right floor.

He'd seen the slight crack in the window on the third left pane and could be certain that in no less than fifteen strides he'd be at the hand sanitiser by the side of the heavy wooden double doors with the blue and white ICU sign posted above.

Pumping the sanitiser with one hand and pressing the buzzer with the other, James waited anxiously for one of the nurses to let him in. There'd just been a shift change over so it was a busy time. When the door clicked open, he didn't stop at the front desk to ask how I was. The receptionist was on the telephone, tapping something into a screen, and nodding sympathetically.

If she had looked up and seen it was James, she could

have warned him. She'd have put a hand up to signal for him to wait just a second while she asked her caller to hold. James rounded the corner and saw four bays, as usual. But my bay was empty. My bed had gone. There was no sign of my belongings, no cards on the shelves, none of mum's books, no monitors beeping or ventilators swooshing.

It was as if I'd been unhooked, dismantled and disposed of just as swiftly and efficiently as if someone had died.

Then it hit him. I was dead.

There'd been another missed call on his phone in the time he was driving, but he hadn't dared answer it. It was mum. He knew now that the phone call had been to tell him that I had died. I was at the morgue. Not to bother going to ICU because I didn't exist anymore.

His legs went from beneath him.

Why had he been at work and not here? Why hadn't mum rung sooner? Where was I?

One of the nurses was catching up with him as he took in the empty space. Luckily, in that short time she'd realised nobody had told James.

She caught his arm as he was falling and guided him into a chair. She explained I wasn't dead, but was in a side room to prevent any infection due to my high temperature.

Mum and dad were with me. It was okay, I wasn't dead. I wasn't dead.

6

·

Institutionalised

MUM AND I HAVE spoken of Dr Doom's prognosis since and about how, if he'd been correct, I wouldn't have wanted to be kept alive.

What sort of an existence can you have if you're a slobbering mess, unable to walk, talk and feed yourself? It's not living and it's not fair to those around you. But being in my early twenties, I hadn't even considered the idea of writing a living will and, as it happened, Dr Doom was wide of the mark.

While the medical team did everything in their power to bring my temperature back down in that side room, my fiancé decided to move out of the hospital and back home.

That was a huge relief to mum and dad, but there was still a very tight rope to walk. He continued to visit me most days, but they tried to time it so there wasn't any crossover. No visual contact.

There'd already been one incident where he and dad nearly came to blows on the ward and the staff asked them to leave. Tempers were frayed on all sides. And *he* hadn't even gone to court yet.

Friends from farther afield were now beginning to pop in, all hoping to be the one who'd finally break my silence or somehow make a connection with me.

The first of my Liverpool paramedic crew to make the journey across the M62 was Graeme, with his wife Gill. What a legend Graeme is.

He's quite tall with short dark hair and at the time had a cracking moustache. He's still pretty lean because even though he's in his sixties now, he competes in a water-polo team at a decent level.

I learned so much working with Graeme – not just the medical aspects of the job, but a lot about how to deal with people. I think he met Gill at the hospital in Liverpool, where she was an ICU nurse. They're a perfect match, both having an ability to put people at their ease immediately. They invited me round to their house a couple times, where I met their gorgeous daughter, Molly.

Well, he rocked up to ICU with a flaming harmonica. It broke the atmosphere, if not my silence.

He said: 'Hi George, I'm going to play the harmonica for you now. I can give you a blow on my organ too if you like. Gill had a blow on my organ on the way up, but she dropped it and broke the vein.'

Apparently, I opened my eyes and looked at him.

He used to take that harmonica everywhere when we were on shift. We once went to a patient who was suffering from severe abdominal pains, so quite difficult to understand. Graeme got his harmonica out, played a quick tune, then asked the patient what he thought. The patient mustered and said: 'I'd rather have the pain in my stomach than listen to you playing that.'

But Graeme had raised a smile, so it did the trick.

I hadn't ever expected that I'd be on the receiving end of one of his serenades and can totally relate to the guy with belly ache now.

One way mum tried to relax in the midst of this hell was by going outside to smoke, to chit-chat to other patients and find out what they were 'in for'.

Dad would have joined her, but he quit his sixty-a-day habit in on New Year's Eve in 1985, after a pact with James. He said he'd never have another cigarette again if James promised to stop biting his fingernails. Both were true to their word. But while mum puffed her stress away in smoker's corner, she got friendly with a homeless guy. God knows what they talked about.

Maybe he made mum feel grateful that I at least had a roof over my head, or maybe he just liked the fact that she used to bung him a few extra Silk Cut for the mornings.

I think her and dad created this little microcosm of a world for a while, just based at the hospital. Theirs had shrunk dramatically and mum, in particular, was beginning to become institutionalised.

Dad had been nipping out occasionally to check in at work, but it was a full six weeks before mum left the hospital grounds. In all that time she'd only been able to have a flannel wash – not even a shower or bath. Fortunately, she was never one to slap on the make-up, so apart from getting paler and thinner over the weeks, she didn't look like one of these women who are unrecognisable without their eyebrows and lip-liner drawn on.

Eventually though, mum's sister Pat put her foot down. She booked a hotel room near the hospital and basically frogmarched my parents there. Pat told them to spend a couple of hours relaxing, having a bath, resting on clean sheets, looking at the TV – basically anything to give them a wider perspective, if just for an afternoon.

There was no way mum would have strayed as far back as home, but she could just about cope with being half a mile away and appreciated the gesture, and they both felt slightly more human afterwards.

Back at Jimmy's, mum and dad became friendly with an Asian family who were also staying in a hospitality room; their daughter was in ICU too.

The rooms were quite small – just enough for two people really – but dad says they often had seven in next door. He said they were so kind and generous, offering mum and dad fruit and other foods. But it all got a bit out of hand because mum and dad returned the favour by getting them some lovely sweets. Then the next day, they returned the favour with a load more sweets. They had to call a friendly truce on offering each other food in the end.

The thing that mum and dad struggled to understand was that this other family wanted to give their poorly daughter a drink of water from the Ganges.

They believed it was holy water and would help her recover. Apparently, you can order this water, known as Gangajal, online and have it posted to your door.

It comes from two main places along the river called Gangotri and Rishikesh and it's only about 20p. I wouldn't fancy it myself though because there are all kinds of reports about the Ganges being badly polluted with industrial waste, sewage and even dead bodies. Needless to say, nobody in the hospital would allow them to give it to their daughter.

The room at the other side of mum and dad's on the ward was also full for a while – but not with people, just flowers. So many well-wishers had sent huge bouquets and baskets that there literally wasn't enough space near my bed. It was a florist's dream. I wish I could have seen them all.

I don't think flowers are permitted in hospitals now because of allergies and infections, which is such a shame. When you do finally come around, and you're flat on your back, there's nothing to see other than life support machines and the ceiling. So even a couple of chrysanthemums would break up the view and raise your spirits.

I'm sure mum and dad's appetites were depleted, but the nurses insisted that they kept themselves properly fed and watered. Sometimes they'd grab a bite downstairs in the café when I had visitors, but eventually they started getting the odd curry delivered from a place nearby, which always arrived with plates, cutlery and napkins for them.

Mum and dad were so impressed because the owner and staff always asked how I was getting on. Subsequently, a few months after being released from Jimmy's, we went to their restaurant. They were brilliant, making sure there was plenty of space for my wheelchair and not tucking us out of the way because I had to be spoon fed.

It was a huge milestone for me, that meal out. But it was sensory overload being in such a different environment to a care-setting.

Although I really appreciated being somewhere – anywhere, frankly – that didn't smell of Dettol, I struggled with my pride.

I'd happily coped with intimate procedures by all and sundry in the months before. Internal examinations of every orifice, help with the bathroom, even wiping my nose, none of that was as excruciating as having to be fed.

I found it acutely embarrassing and hated myself for feeling that way. But the experience served to make me even more determined to be independent. I just felt that there was no way I could remain like this for the rest of my life. I was willing to do whatever it took to get myself back on track. My only major stumbling block then – and now – is impatience.

So even though I was in no fit state to be contemplating the minutiae of my future at that point, I don't think any of us could have guessed that I'd be writing an email like this in 2016:

To: Unique Pole Fitness
From: Georgina Hurst

Dear Hayley,
Can spastics pole dance?
I was in a car accident eighteen years ago which left me with limited use of my legs. Most of the time I use a wheelchair, but I can get about on crutches if I don't have far to go.
Could you help me?
Yours hopefully,
George

Hayley responded that same day:

Dear George,
I'm really sorry to hear about your accident, but it sounds like you've got a real fighting spirit and I'd love to be able to help. Let's give it a shot. What's the worst that can happen?
Best wishes,
Hayley

Well, quite.

Unbroken

The worst already had happened, and I'd recovered.

I loved that she was willing to take a chance on me, so I replied with a suggested date and that was the beginning. Over the period of four years, we became good friends and she helped me achieve innumerable pole fitness goals. Hayley became one of the many people who guided me along the road to becoming a fitter, happier person.

When a friend showed *him* the pictures on Facebook from my pole dancing photoshoot, *his* face dropped. I was upside down, in a leather basque, looking hot as hell.

Many years ago, I'd have wanted him to see that picture and want me. Now, I honestly couldn't care less. Particularly now everything has come to light about what he was up to while I was in hospital.

7
•
State of Awareness

MUM'S SURPRISED THAT I can remember her reading *The Horse Whisperer* to me because I was constantly drifting in and out of sleep.

But by that time, I'd graduated from ICU and on to Ward 24 at Jimmy's, so I can't have been completely out of it. The story got into my head somehow.

I couldn't have made up exactly the same tale, with exactly the same title, can I? It was really comforting to know mum was there though. Reassuring.

She could have been reading absolutely anything and I'd have loved it. Well, I might have tried to communicate a bit sooner if she'd started on Shakespeare's sonnets, just so I could tell her to stop.

It's funny though, I don't remember *him* ever reading to me. And he would have had plenty of time to do so because his court case wasn't until the following April – eight months after he nearly killed me. I wasted a lot of time wishing he was by my bedside, I genuinely looked forward to seeing him. But even when he was there, he wasn't really there. He was going through the motions, probably wondering how on earth he was going to cope with the inevitability of jail and a life with me, like this.

When I emerged from the induced coma – a full seven weeks after the accident – I couldn't talk. One factor was because I still had a tracheostomy fitted.

That's where they make a small incision in your neck to your trachea and insert a tube so you can breathe without using your nose or mouth. It's one step closer to breathing on your own after a full ventilator.

It looks a bit like a choker made for someone who's into surgical sadomasochism. Now, this is a weird side note – perhaps it was the drugs at the time, but one of the things I used to love, was when the nurse came to check the trachea was clear of phlegm and nastiness by ramming a little rod down it. That's not normal is it?

I think there was something about the relief of knowing I'd definitely be able to breathe again properly. Or maybe it was just as simple as relieving the boredom.

The other reason I couldn't speak after being brought out of the coma was the result of my broken neck, which had partially paralysed my throat at the back.

If mum was by my bedside and she wasn't reading, there was still no chance of any peace and quiet for me.

She felt the need to constantly prattle on about all the comings and goings on the ward, fully aware of the fact that when people appear unconscious, they can still hear.

She used to make up names for people. She'd be like: 'Ooh, here comes hop-along with the funny nose,' or 'There's the Charity Shop clothes queen.'

I do wonder if it was ever really necessary to put me in that side room when I had a temperature spike. Perhaps they just wanted to close the door on mum's musings.

Once I was in a state of awareness, but still nowhere near able to move, it felt like everything was occurring around me. I just allowed things happen.

There seemed to be so many doctors and nurses coming and going, checking and re-checking, doling out medicines, dressing my wounds, adjusting my bed, my blankets, my body. And of course, I was still trying to come to terms with why I was in hospital in the first place.

That's one of the first things a patient has to be told – what happened to get them into this state. It's so they're not frightened, but it has to be done in a very basic, matter of fact way. Not too much information but enough, delivered calmly. It's very common to have to be told again and again over weeks, sometimes months, because your brain is still playing catch-up, your short-term memory is shot, and you immediately forget.

Also, people often don't believe what they're being told, or can't comprehend it. And sometimes, your brain tries to shield you from the truth. I was told simply that I'd been in a car accident and I was now being looked after in Jimmy's hospital in Leeds.

It obviously took a long time to sink in. Even longer for me to get to a stage where I could somehow communicate to mum how I felt about it. But when I did, far from being sympathetic towards me, I received a full and frank rollocking. Not about *him* or the crash, but about my attitude towards what was going to happen next. I had to be strong, not ever say 'what if?' and never look back.

I was told I had to make the best of what I had, that my future was different, but not worse. In short, I just had to get better and get on with it. Cope with the hand I'd been unexpectedly dealt.

I took that on board as much as I could. Laid there recovering from a broken neck, shattered pelvis, broken leg, torn liver, kidneys and bladder and two punctured lungs, I made myself think: 'Right, what next?'

There was no chance to wallow, no time allowed in our conversations to contemplate what might have been. Regret wasn't optional.

It might sound harsh, but I know it was coming from the right place with mum. She didn't want to see me sad, she needed me to fight so she could get her old George back.

She'd been brought up like many in her generation to move on with a stiff upper lip. Head down, bum up, get on with it. Her and dad the same. It's what they still do to this day.

I couldn't think too far ahead. I had no idea if I'd be able to walk again. There was no time frame for me. I just had to try and make myself believe that at some point, everything would be alright. That if I focussed on what was possible in the short term, I might be able to set my sights on longer term goals eventually.

As I couldn't move, it seemed obvious to me that the first thing I needed to do was learn to talk again. Or at least convey more clearly exactly what I was thinking.

That became my priority. I could hear, but I desperately needed some two-way interaction. I'll be honest, my voice still really bothers me now.

It was one of the first things that came up in my initial session with my psychotherapist, Catherine. I told her that I hate sounding like a tit. She doesn't like that I'm so harsh on myself, so it's something we're going to work through together.

It's taken a long time to get my speech to this level. I'm at a stage now where people can usually understand me, but I still find it demoralising when they can't get the gist immediately.

It's annoying too, but a lot better than being one of those people who are 'locked in' for their whole lives. It must be torture to understand everything but be able to say nothing.

I wonder how many people there have been like Stephen Hawking, before the brilliance of technology enabled them to have a voice again? All those clever minds gone to waste – those thoughts never spoken and feelings never shared.

I am so, so grateful that I found mine again and don't have to rely on a computerised app to convey my emotions.

It wasn't just the accident that caused issues with my speech, it was afterwards too, when I had to be ventilated. They caught my larynx, my vocal chords – or voice box as it's commonly known.

Add to that the fact that my palate was partially paralysed due to my broken neck and you've got a two-pronged nightmare.

When most people speak, they naturally close off the back of their throat to create sounds, but mine can't do that to the same degree, which is why I sound strained.

But the feeling in my palate has mainly returned now and it's as good as it's going to get, thanks to a mouth guard I wore in hospital to help correct it, so I just have to work with what I've got.

I had speech therapy for a while and got to a certain, basic level, but the first therapist said: 'You'll never improve.' What? How ridiculous. I know I've improved. I'm not brilliant, but I'm definitely better.

Initially my voice was all one tone, and I couldn't really shout. But now inflection isn't as much of a problem. You'd know if I was being sarcastic or if I was angry.

It's still frustrating that I think a lot quicker than I can sometimes speak and when I'm tired I slur a bit too, which can give the impression I've been on the bubbly.

I tried another two or three speech therapists after that initial experience, but I think that's me done now. I can ring people and they generally know what I'm talking about.

I've learned to acknowledge my voice at the start of telephone conversations with people I haven't met before. I explain that I kind-of broke my voice box and that's why I sound like I've got a sore throat and speak slower.

It helps too when I say I'd rather hear 'pardon' a thousand times than them pretend to comprehend what I've said. That whole spiel only takes about a minute, but it makes a huge difference to the direction of the rest of the call.

Other people's embarrassment is often the cause of a lot of misunderstanding and unnecessary angst.

I was filmed in the early stages of my speech therapy and looking back at those old VHS tapes now makes me realise how far I've come.

The best way to improve my voice is to use it and fortunately, I've always got something to say. I suppose I can't be too bad because I'm invited all over the place to speak about my recovery.

Those old tapes also came in very handy years later when my nephew, Brennan, was learning to drive. My brother wanted to show him what might happen to him if he drove like an idiot. It's just a shame I looked such a chubster in the videos. And my hair was an abomination.

But showing Brennan was a stroke of genius. Not much longer after that, he was the passenger in his friend's car and his friend was speeding and showing off. Apparently, Brennan turned to him and said: 'Either slow down or let me out,' then reminded him about me. Who knows, perhaps I inadvertently saved another life or two?

Before I could talk at all though, mum, dad and James all came up with ideas to create some kind of system so that I could let them know what I wanted to say.

James made a board with the alphabet on – he'd seen it done somewhere else before – and suggested I blink when he pointed to the letters or words.

Mum suggested saying the alphabet out loud, then I could stick my tongue out when it got to the letter I wanted. Saying it out loud seemed to work the best at the time, so that's how we started.

It made for some very long conversations. Then we made it quicker by splitting the alphabet into two, so she would start with either A or L and go from there. Once we got the hang of it, there was no stopping us. We had lift off.

Mum, characteristically, really persevered with this system. She wanted to prove to people that I still had everything going on upstairs, that just because I didn't look in great form physically, didn't mean my brain had been smashed up too.

She had me doing spelling tests. It was like being a child again, when James and I were at the same primary school where mum was a teacher.

It reminded me of how she'd always be checking our sums and spellings as she drove us there in our old orange polo, which we nicknamed RV Olop.

The name came about because the registration plate had the letters RV in it and Olop is Polo spelled backwards.

I'm glad mum wasn't our form teacher though because she was so strict, not that it stopped James from winding her up. At school one day he was obviously acting up in front of his friends – testing the boundaries. We'd all filed into the dinner hall for morning assembly.

A faint whiff of corned beef pie and cabbage came from the kitchen at the back, our bare legs crossed on the cold hard floor. Boy-girl-boy-girl, to avoid any rowdiness; everybody leaning over each other, chattering away.

Then mum marched in, her dark perm bouncing just above her shoulders, and asked us to stand.

'Good morning, children' she said.

'Good moor-ning Miss-iz Hurst,' we parroted.

Mum took her place behind the lectern and began. I've honestly no idea what she was talking about, but she was in full flow until she heard whistling. At that, she paused and said: 'Whoever is whistling, please stop now.' So it stopped. Then mum began again and so did the whistling.

She was getting crosser and crosser until, eventually, she just yelled: 'James Hurst, I know it's you and if you don't stop at once, you'll get a smacked bottom.' That shut him up. Fortunately her patience and hard work in our primary years – and then latterly, with me in hospital – paid off.

One of my favourite Jimmy's moments was when mum returned from grabbing a coffee in the canteen downstairs. She plonked the cup on my bedside table, looked me in the eye and asked if anyone else had been on the ward to see me while she'd been gone.

I spelled out: 'p h y s i o t h e r a p i s t.'

Sometimes though, communicating seemed so much hassle, especially in the early days when my friends came to visit. What could I have to say of any interest that they didn't already know from my parents and the doctors anyway? Er, I'm still here? I've had soup for lunch?

To begin with, I preferred it when they did the talking

and updated me on what was going on in their lives. Two of my most regular visitors, who always brought news and a bit of laughter, were Bingley Grammar School friends Vick and Andrea (Andi).

Those two were at my bedside within the very first few days of the crash and are part of our wider group which includes Alycia, Bee, Nicola and Fern.

We'd all somehow gravitated towards each other in our second year at school through the usual common interests: boys, plus the happenstance of being in the same classes or living nearby. They were much nicer than the bunch I'd met in my first year, who were basically bullying mean girls.

Vick was probably what you'd call our 'group leader'. Confident, pretty, popular, clever and captain of the netball team. In our final year she was head girl, which suited her highly organised personality. She had a lovely olive complexion and long dark hair which was often pulled back into a swishy ponytail.

Most of the boys fancied her and most of the girls fancied her older brother. Looking back, I'm not entirely sure what we had in common, but history keeps you connected.

I'd say Andi was more on my level academically, but equally as attractive as Vick. Similar coloured hair but tinier features and, although she's great fun to be around, probably not as out-going. But the two of them really stuck together and helped each other a lot after my crash.

Unbelievably sadly, Andi's boyfriend was also in hospital at the same time as me, but twenty-three miles away, over in Halifax. Only two months after I was admitted, he lost his battle with motor neurone disease.

Prior to my accident, Vick had been working in London and not really enjoying her job. Andi was helping her mum with her extremely busy catering business, while trying to spend as much time with her boyfriend as she could. But Andi couldn't drive and so when news reached Vick of my crash, Vick simply jacked in her job and drove back up north.

She spent her time filling in for Andi at the catering business, then driving herself and Andi to see me one day, then Andi's boyfriend the next. It was full-on for both of them, but they still found time to make things as cheery as possible.

Once, they brought in a huge Spice Girls poster for my wall, which they'd cut the faces out of and replaced with photos of all of us instead.

They played Take That music on a portable CD player and read out terrible jokes from a joke book. I still love a bad joke. In fact, I still love Take That too and, years later, we all went to see them perform at the Birmingham NEC.

8

•

Not So Great Expectations

YOU DON'T REALISE how popular you are until you've returned from the brink of death. The good friends I'd made at Nab Wood middle school, Tracy, Emma and Fern, were eager to see me too.

Fern really made me laugh when she reminded me of the time we both put tennis racket covers on our heads and danced around her bedroom to the TV theme tune of *Pinky and Perky*.

It was so funny and innocent. Little memories like that can give you a lot of joy when you're just stuck in a hospital bed with nothing else to think about. It makes you look forward to feeling well again.

When their visit was over, my mind drifted further back to when James was about six and I dressed him up in some of my clothes and mum's lipstick, then made him walk to the neighbour's house to see if he could pass as a girl.

Unbroken

I'm not sure he's ever forgiven me for that, but he got his own back plenty of times when we played armies and I was always the captured German awaiting torture.

All my other paramedic work pals came to visit me in Jimmy's too, including my best work buddy, Caroline.

Caroline was a great team player out on the road, but once she clocked off, the pair of us shared some really wild nights out in Liverpool. Her boyfriend was a mafia-type in charge of all the bouncers, so we could just breeze into the decent bars and clubs without queuing or paying.

It also helped that she was stunning, so attracted plenty of attention – and we both loved to dance. Neither of us ever took it steady on the Snakebite, so we've seen each other in some right states, but this probably took the biscuit.

She must have thought my disco days were well and truly over seeing me held together by metalwork, silenced. It's fair to say she was absolutely gobsmacked when she heard of my pole dancing antics nearly two decades later.

Word of my crash reached right to the top of the ambulance service and even the head honcho at the time, David Todhunter, paid me a visit.

He was known as a real tough nut, but was so taken aback when he saw me surrounded by all the cards and flowers that he actually cried. There and then he pledged to pay for a minibus for any colleagues who wanted to visit me at any time.

And when I was well enough, he arranged for me to go back and see the team again. Graeme says it's just as well I had the accident in Yorkshire; had I been in Liverpool, I wouldn't have got a minute's rest, with so many people popping in between shifts.

My job was held open for me for a long time and they looked at all kinds of alternatives to keep me on the payroll

– but the reality was that I couldn't work again at that point. I still couldn't hold down a full-time job now, not really. I wouldn't even feel confident answering the phone on the call desk, because people on the other line with an emergency might mis-hear instructions:

Me: 'You need to clear their airway and turn them onto their side.'

What they'd hear: 'I've weed in the stairway and died.'

And because of my dexterity issues, I can't lift and shift – which is quite a large part of the job.

It wasn't just the medical side of things I loved as a paramedic but the humanity of it. It was life as well as death.

During my time in Liverpool, I helped deliver four healthy babies into the world and there's nothing like it. It's such a privilege to be part of something so special.

Graeme, having been in the job much longer than me, has sadly seen a handful of baby deaths, each one of which is unforgettable in its own tragic way. But after one incident, when he returned to the station needing a quiet moment, it was one of the cleaners who made him a sweet tea and sat to talk.

The NHS team is so much wider than just your immediate colleagues. Every single person working for the National Health Service makes a difference.

Camaraderie and banter are also essential tools when working in the emergency services. Obviously, you know when you have to be ultra-serious, but for some of the shall-we-say 'stranger' call outs, I could just about hold it together until out of sight and earshot.

Once, Graeme and I had to go to a house with 'invisible' people. The patient was having hallucinations and refused to come out of their home until all the 'other' people had left. We had to go round each room, pretending to kick them out. It was like: 'I've got one Graeme, can you give me a hand?' or 'This one's happy to leave on his own accord, I'll just leave the door ajar for him.' Once the patient thought everybody was out of his house, he came with us. But you just have to go along with it.

Graeme didn't know this at the time, but not long before the crash I'd applied for a job with West Yorkshire Ambulance Service (WYAS). It was to do exactly the same thing, but it meant I'd be nearer home – or more specifically, nearer *him*.

I'd been a bit nervous about finding the place where my interview was held, so the evening prior Alycia had come with me to find the location.

We did a trial run so it was one less thing to worry about on the day. I thought the interview went quite well and was just waiting to hear back from them. Weeks after my accident, WYAS contacted mum. They'd sent me an acceptance letter and wondered why I hadn't responded.

Mum had the dreadful task of not only filling them in on what had happened but, when I was ready, telling me. It was a bitter-sweet news. Obviously, it was a real confidence boost that I'd been offered the job, but it really brought home the magnitude of my situation.

I would have had a job I loved, in a place I called home, with a man I was going to marry. And even though I really hoped on some level that I'd recover enough to accept the position, I knew deep down that was never going to happen.

It had taken me such a long time to figure out what I'd really wanted to do with my life and now I couldn't bloody well do it. It was galling to say the least.

I'd never been top of the class at school – but I was far from thick. I got a clutch of average GCSEs and went on to do 'A' levels, but preferred the social life to lessons so pretty much scraped by. I could have done better if I'd applied myself, but I'd recently learned to drive so often nipped home when my parents were at work – sometimes with my boyfriend. Say no more. Sorry, mum.

On results day, when my friends had places confirmed at various universities, I went through a system called clearing with the University and Colleges Admissions Service and took the first course to accept my grades – Hotel Management and Catering at Stafford college. I lasted a year.

Parts of my time in Stafford were great. I lived with two other girls, Helen and Mabel, who were both my age. I knew I was going to get on with Helen straight away when she admitted her geography was so bad she thought we were in Stratford and wondered why nothing seemed 'Shakespeary'.

She was lovely, really kind and funny, with layered sandy hair falling just below her shoulders. She was a size-twelve jeans-and-docs girl, usually twinning them with floaty, tasseled tops over her big boobs.

We had a lot of laughs together, either mucking about in the house, clubbing or even just going to the cinema.

I remember we scared ourselves stupid watching *Silence of the Lambs* when that came out. Basically, she was just very easy company, and I could see why her boyfriend Phil adored her.

Mabel was different. She was a goth, so often dressed in black, highlighting her pale skin with dark eyeliner. Her long curly fringe almost reached down to her pieced nose and her pinched, skinny features called attention to her nutritionally barren diet.

To be fair, she was friendly enough at first, but I soon realised she blew hot and cold. She was the type of person who'd be best friends with you one minute before ignoring you the next. In a good mood, you'd be the centre of her world but on an off day, completely blanked. She'd join in but it was always on her terms or she simply wouldn't bother. Nobody could have predicted what she'd do just before Christmas though.

Stafford is quite a big university town, but the house I lived in with Helen and Mabel was just north of it, away from the student area. It was a 1940s end-terrace with an Esso garage nearby and basic to say the least. A bit moldy due to no central heating and home to a handful of mice, which dad trapped and poisoned on a mercy mission after I found one of them, headless, under my pillow.

There was nothing as luxurious as a telephone landline, so if we wanted to call home we had to use the payphone at the garage. None of us had mobiles at that point.

I knew the course wasn't for me though and spent more hours in a pub called Crispins than I did in the classroom.

It was one of these big, towny bars with a room at the back where they had functions. The sort of place where, if you'd been brought up in the area, you'd have your wedding reception, christening and wake. Discos every weekend, quizzes during the week, one step up from a meat raffle pub. I literally just walked in and asked Barbara the landlady for a job and got one. I also managed to get Helen and Mabel work too. It was quite a novelty for the punters to have three students behind the bar.

It wasn't long before I spotted – and snared – the fittest guy in the pub. He was the resident DJ.

Christian was a few years older than me, about twenty-one, medium height, shaved head and popular with the locals, a bit of a joker, not exactly a jack-the-lad, but everyone knew him and he played the music I loved from the early 90s, like The Wonder Stuff's 'Dizzy' and 'Sit Down' by James.

He mixed it up with a bit of Depeche Mode too, for the

slightly older clientele. I really liked him at the time, probably even thought I loved him, but in hindsight I think I was probably more enamored with the fact that he'd chosen me above anyone else.

The first few months in Stafford were good fun. I was hardly a model student, but I embraced my new-found freedom and when I did turn up to lessons had a giggle with Helen, particularly during the practical work where we were forced to wear hideous catering uniforms to serve in the college restaurant.

It was good to be meeting new people and earning a bit of spending money. I was happy just pinballing from the pub to Christian, figuring I'd get the first year done then make a proper plan after that. But towards the end of November I was in a bit of a pickle. I hadn't noticed my period was a couple of weeks late, until my hangovers expanded from headaches to nagging nausea.

Pregnancy tests were pricey back then, plus I wanted to speak to a doctor about my options. I knew I wasn't ready to be a mother and presumed it would be Christian's worst nightmare to become a young dad. There was no way I could carry a child and then give it up for adoption, so there really was only one path to take.

The doctor was very sympathetic, not a bit judgmental. The first thing she did was pack me off to the toilet with a test, just to be sure.

When I returned with my wee stick, she confirmed my suspicions and talked me through the possible scenarios.

She said there was no rush. I was very early on, barely even a cluster of cells taking shape, but I'd made my mind up before I even walked through the door. I knew if I was definitely pregnant, I wanted a termination asap.

Even though I knew it was the right decision I felt

extremely vulnerable. Part of it was probably due to the massive surge in hormones raging round my body, but I thought if I confided in Christian, he'd support me and we could get through it together.

I was wrong.

It's not that he wanted the child, he just didn't want anything to do with the process. In a nutshell, I had an abortion alone. There was so much going through my mind. It was hard dealing with the logistics and looking back, I should maybe have told Helen.

I'm sure she would have held my hand through it all. But for some reason I didn't want anyone to know. On some level I thought that if I didn't talk about it, I could pretend it hadn't happened and just get back to normal. I couldn't be reminded of something if nobody else knew about it. But by keeping it all in, my brain somehow chose to trigger that memory hinted at earlier in these pages, from when I was fourteen. The shock of the recollection blindsided me.

I thought I'd done a great job of well and truly burying the incident, but when echoes of the horror emerged again, the weight, on top of my current crisis, threatened to engulf me. Everything felt black. I assumed that it was my body re-adjusting to the sudden exit of hormones and wondered if anti-depressants might temporarily be the answer.

After all, you'd take a pill for a physical pain, so why not mental turmoil? I made another appointment with the doctor, but didn't give her the full story.

To my mind, it didn't matter to her what the cause of my dark cloud was, just that there was one. All I told her was that I was struggling a bit coming to terms with the abortion and I was unhappy at college. That's all that was needed for a prescription.

I'd been taking the anti-depressants for about two

weeks. I hadn't told mum and dad I was on them, nor had I told them about my abortion.

I think that was part of the problem, keeping everything bottled up, plastering a smile on my face while feeling helpless inside, stuck in a fog of not knowing what or who I wanted. I couldn't think straight and needed to escape from all the emotions swooshing around my head.

There didn't seem to be a specific moment when I was galvanised into action. The whole thing just crept up on me like it was the only way I could see of being able to exorcise my demons.

I hadn't thought about the effect it might have on anybody else, the devastation I could cause by taking my own life, because I was too far into my own head for a wider perspective. Slipping away from it all felt like such an appealing idea and so I found myself in the kitchen with a glass of water and the rest of my anti-depressants.

I pushed down and unscrewed the child protection cap, shaking out the first bunch of white capsules into the palm of my hand. Staring at them, I wondered what each one contained and how many I'd need before oblivion.

Tipping as many as I could into my mouth, I reached for the glass with my other hand, bringing the rim to my lips, my front teeth clanging against it, then gulped them down.

More tablets – hand to mouth, glass to lips, not long now. I was desperate not to feel.

Even though I was shaking I felt calmer inside because I was taking control – or so I thought. I wiped my mouth dry with my sleeve and leaned against the chipped pale blue Formica worktop, waiting for something to happen.

I hadn't considered what it would feel like to die, if it would hurt, whether I'd feel sick, dizzy or hallucinate. Tablets simply equaled a way out right then.

Staring into space in the deathly quiet house I suddenly needed fresh air and had to be outside. I don't know why, maybe I had to tell someone what I'd done.

Trying to recollect events now, it is feelings rather than actions that come back. I'd been cold, I remember that much, but don't recall putting my coat on, or shoes for that matter. I just assume that I did.

I have hazy flashbacks of passing houses in our street, catching glimpses through windows of Christmas trees adorned with twinkling lights and tinsel, spray snow in the corners. Other windows were dark, nobody home, a bit like how it was within my mind.

It's hard for me to talk about this publicly because other than a few close friends and family, not many people know. But recently, I told the basics to my therapist and she thinks it is something else we ought to look at together.

There is a lot to unravel about my attempted suicide, because the pieces of the jigsaw still don't quite fit.

Somehow, I found myself back in the tiny galley kitchen of our student house, where Mabel, my goth friend, stood near the door. She lurched towards me, thrusting the empty bottle of tablets up to my face and shouted: 'What have you done, George? What have you done?'

I couldn't answer, I just felt blank.

But instead of trying to help me, to make me sick or call an ambulance, she began taunting me, grabbing a packet of paracetamol from the cupboard and urged me to take more if I really meant it.

I watched her pushing the pills through the foil blister packet, passing them to me one after another, filling the glass of water, saying: 'Go on then. Do it if you really mean it. Do it.' And I just complied, robotic-like, calmly swallowing and gulping my way out of there.

I still don't understand it. I knew she was odd, but I'm sure we hadn't fallen out. Was she calling my bluff? Or was she psychotic? Why would she do that?

Then the next thing I knew, I was in a hospital and mum and dad were there, along with my Auntie Pat and Uncle Alan, my parents having raced down the M6 in the fog, ringing Pat and Alan before they set off as they lived quite near to Stafford, in Lichfield.

Dad had taken the phone call from the hospital – he'd been told to get there asap. I'd had my stomach pumped – but I can't remember that. That's just what they told me.

I still don't know who called the ambulance. Could it have been Mabel? Maybe she frightened herself and called 999, then disappeared.

Or was it me at the petrol station, after I'd taken the anti-depressants, but before the paracetamol? I don't think so. I think I'd have remembered that.

Helen wasn't there because she'd gone home – it was the start of the Christmas holidays – Friday 13 December, bizarrely; and dad can't remember who rang him from the hospital.

When I came around, I was an emotional wreck, but relieved it hadn't worked. I think it was a cry for help because I just clung to mum and let everything out about Christian and the termination.

She hugged me, reassuring me everything would be okay, that I'd get through it and needed to come home for Christmas. She said I must never get myself into that state again, but talk to her if I was ever feeling down. I was offered a counsellor at the hospital but, once I'd told mum, just wanted to put it all behind me.

Mum understood. She was really good, a true friend. I stayed with her and dad until the start of the next academic term in January. It was never mentioned in the house in Stafford, and because Helen wasn't there at the time, it came as a real shock to her when I told her years later.

I went back to work at Crispins, but Christian and I drifted. We were more friends-with-benefits after that really.

I stopped going to classes altogether and, when the first year of the course drew to a close, my tutors knew as well as I did that my heart wasn't in the course, so I left.

Back home that summer I saw an advert for au pairs in America. Having no better plan in mind, I filled out an application form and after a telephone interview, was found a family.

That September I boarded a flight to Virginia, where I was met by a couple and their children and driven to a very fancy gated housing community called Aquia Harbour in the suburbs of a place that was coincidentally called Stafford County. It was during my spare time there that I volunteered for the community's medical emergency crew.

They took me under their wing and put me through basic training. That's when I knew I had found my 'thing'.

9

•

Renewed Strength

AFTER THE CRASH, I began to grasp what had happened to me. My thoughts turned to my appearance. I knew my body didn't feel great and the penny was dropping that I wouldn't be skipping out of Jimmy's any time soon.

I could see that my pelvis was bolted together and I knew my head was in a halo, but I didn't know what state my face was in.

I imagined that I had a lot of scarring, that my jaw was probably misshapen and that my ears, for some reason, were lopsided. It sounds vain, but I honestly didn't know.

I couldn't lift my hands up to feel my face. It was physically impossible to move my fingers over my cheeks, my nose, my lips, to get a mental image of the damage caused and I realised nobody was saying anything.

I tried to remember comments from friends and family in terms of my appearance, but all I could recall were generic phrases like: 'You're looking better,' 'You're on the mend,' or talk would be of injuries I could see myself, like my hips.

I began to believe that everyone was just being kind and that, really, I was a horror from the neck up.

My short-term memory still wasn't great, but I was at least getting to grips with communicating by sticking my tongue out. Three months after the accident I plucked up the courage to cobble together the words to ask mum: 'What does my face look like?' Mum felt dreadful and still feels guilty about not realising sooner that it was bothering me. But it's not like she didn't have anything else to think about.

I can't blame her, given how she was still wondering whether or not I'd even be able to walk or talk. We're all so used to seeing ourselves in the mirror we don't give it a second thought.

From the minute we wake up and clean our teeth, to before we go to bed, there are mirrors everywhere – cars, shop windows, at the hairdresser's, in our wardrobe doors. We check our reflections so many times without realising it.

But once mum knew I wanted to see my face, she went to find a mirror straight away and, after realising there was nothing on the ward, made her way to the newsagent's on the hospital ground floor.

It had a couple of shelves for people who'd been rushed in with no time to pack an overnight bag, offering overpriced bars of soap, flannels, toothbrushes, shower caps, lip balm and even packs of pyjamas. At the back of the top shelf, she spotted a small handbag-style mirror, the folding sort which closes with a clasp, housing blusher and brush or a second, magnifying mirror to make you feel bad about your blackheads.

She took it to the counter, along with a newspaper she'd save for reading later while I was sleeping. The front page led with Tony Blair becoming the first UK Prime Minister to address the Irish Parliament and BBC confirmation that Patsy Palmer was to leave *EastEnders*.

Walking back along the corridors with her purchases, steeling herself, I saw her turn the corner to my ward and for the first time noticed she looked apprehensive.

Placing the newspaper on the side table, she pulled up a chair, sat down and gently tried to prepare me for what I was about to see.

She said that the halo wouldn't always be there, the swelling would eventually subside and my hair could be styled again. She wanted me to know that I wasn't going to be looking at a reflection of the same George from earlier that year but that, over time, the old me would re-emerge.

I was impatient. I didn't want to hear the preamble. I just wanted to see for myself, but couldn't tell her to just flaming well get on with it.

I needed to do this now and stared at mum, willing her to stop talking and start showing me my reflection. Eventually, she ran out of words, unclasped the mirror and slowly raised it to my face. I burst into tears.

I simply couldn't believe it. The rest of my body was in absolute shreds, but there wasn't so much as a scratch on my chin. My face was bloated, but unscarred. My hair was greasy and limp, but still on my head – only marginally better than my wet-look perm with scraped up sides when I was fifteen.

My ears were in the same place, I had all my teeth and my nose hadn't moved a millimetre. Admittedly, the head brace was a shock – I couldn't believe how alien it looked – but I knew it was only temporary.

I wept with relief. Hot tears escaped and melted into my swollen but unharmed cheeks. I'd got it all wrong in my head. My face was fine. It was fine.

It's hard to explain that feeling. I couldn't move from the neck down, or up, but I was so grateful for that one part of my body which remained unscathed.

It was the proof I needed that I was still me. Behind the frame was a face I recognised as my own and it gave me a renewed strength to do whatever I had to do to get well and get the hell out of hospital.

Mum couldn't understand why I was crying at first. With one hand she continued to hold up the mirror and with the other she was scrabbling for tissues in her handbag.

When she located a scraggy Kleenex, she lowered the mirror and began to dab at my face, turning hers away so as not to see me upset.

My tears kept falling, mixing with salty snot as I tried to catch my breath. I could see mum was trying to hold herself together and thought she must think the halo had freaked me out, so I tried to keep her gaze. I desperately wanted mum to see that I was smiling. That I was happy.

Finally, she rested the tissue on her lap and looked at me properly, confusion in her eyes. I was actually grinning.

It was the first time mum had seen me smile since the accident and the first time I'd seen her well up with joy – ever.

She suddenly knew she'd done the right thing by letting me look in the mirror. I stuck my tongue out to signal that I wanted to say something and she pulled herself together. Slowly, I spelled 'thank you.' We must have looked like a right pair of goons. Mother and daughter just grinning at each other, in hospital.

Happiness can be an exhausting business so, still smiling, I allowed myself to close my eyes and just savour the moment. I sensed mum sit back and pick up her newspaper and I let the soundscape drift over me, feeling safe and hopeful, at peace.

When I awoke, it took a few moments for me to remember about my face, but as the images from the mirror sharpened in my mind again, I began to think about *him*.

Foolishly, it gave me hope that he might still fancy me, that I wasn't going to repulse him for the rest of our lives. He might not look for someone prettier.

That's how insecure I was in our relationship, something inside always telling me I wasn't good enough. After everything he'd done, I still just wanted him to love me.

I'm not proud of this thought, but I hope you can understand it: I'd have found life much harder if I'd been left looking like the Elephant Man.

It would have been the first thing people noticed about me and I'd have hated the staring. I mean, people stare now, but when I'm on my crutches they just see that I struggle to walk, perhaps look at my legs. I'm not embarrassed about that. But with my voice being how it is, it's natural for people to focus on my lips or facial expression to fill in the gaps and I'm not sure how I'd have coped.

In general, I let children get away with ogling when I'm in a wheelchair or on crutches, because they're just curious and often don't know any better.

But if I catch an adult gawping, I let them do it for a while then give them something to stare at. I mysteriously develop a disabled twitch, or if that doesn't send their eyes elsewhere, I feign Tourette's syndrome. My last resort is an 'uncontrollable' kick.

It's common for people who've had life-altering injuries to mentally bargain with fate, or weigh up outcomes from alternative scenarios.

For me, if I'd had to choose between having a facial disfigurement but an able body, or a perfect face and the body I have now, I'd choose what I've got, one hundred per cent.

This way round, I can make improvements. I can work on my physical ability and get as strong as possible, but there are limits to what plastic surgery can do to correct your face.

They said I'd never walk again but I proved everybody wrong. I'm walking with crutches, but I'm still walking and getting fitter every day.

But what if I'd lost part of my nose, my chin or even my eyesight? Not being able to see on top of everything else would have been more that I could have handled. I know it.

Just a few inches either way in terms of impact with the other car and I could have been in a much, much worse state.

I am truly grateful for the small mercy.

10

•

On the Move Again

IT TOOK NEARLY four months for me to make enough progress to be able to leave Jimmy's hospital and move to a convalescence unit on the outskirts of Leeds city centre.

I'd done the best part of eight weeks in ICU before graduating to Ward 24 for another two months. It was a slow process, but certain milestones had to be reached before I could even be considered for release.

My bones and my neck needed to be more stable. I had to prove I could take a small amount of food and drink orally and they needed to ensure I had all my marbles.

The first part of this scrutiny involved an MRI scan – a tip-to-toe X-ray taken in a high-tech piece of kit resembling a crematorium incinerator.

From my trolley bed, I was wheeled down to the radiology department and gently transferred across onto another, longer platform attached to the scanner where, positioned on my back, I was slowly drawn into Hades, head-first.

The little remote-control panic button they'd squeezed into my hand did nothing to allay my rising claustrophobia, but I could relax, they said, because the tiny camera two inches above my face would let them know if I was on the brink of a full-blown panic attack.

Fortunately, the sheer din of whirring and buzzing took my mind off feeling like a cadaver in a coffin and I forced my thoughts away from being buried alive to lounging on a sunbed in Sorrento.

I was in there for what felt like an eternity, but it can't have been more than forty-five minutes. When the clattering ceased and I was released back into the land of the living it felt marvellous, like I could breathe again.

Fortunately, it was all worth it because, later that day, I was told my neck had healed and I could have the halo removed. Thank God for that.

I couldn't wait to feel free around my head and not be constantly itchy around my torso. The solid vest which the halo rods were attached to, had a sheepskin lining for comfort but it often irritated my skin. After having my hair washed, tiny droplets of water made their way down my back, settling on the fleece, turning it prickly as they dried.

Luckily, mum noticed it was making me uncomfortable early on, so worked with the nurses to change the linings regularly, but it was a bug bear. Knowing I was about to be itch-free was almost as good as knowing my neck was healed.

Surprisingly, you don't need pain relief when a halo is removed and it's only supposed to take about ten minutes. It ended up being a job and a half with me and something my dad struggles to forget. When the nurse had tried to loosen the screws into my skull, one of them wouldn't budge. There was an issue with the angle it had initially been inserted behind my ear.

I felt really vulnerable as she tried to gently jimmy it this way and that, my neck being pulled forward with the effort. I knew my neck wasn't broken anymore, but I was just so used to being completely stationary that I worried my vertebrae might not be able to hold my head up.

Dad had half an eye on me, keeping me calm, and another on the struggling nurse. Finally, she managed to ease out the final piece and the whole thing was lifted off.

It felt so strange. I was light-headed at first, but that could have been from the horrific smell. All the time I'd been wearing the halo, I hadn't been able to turn over in bed, so the back of my head had been mainly on the pillow and a small patch of flesh had rotted.

Even though I'd enjoyed having my hair washed, it was very difficult to dry it properly, so the lingering dampness had helped the area decline into a matted, slimy mess. Once the halo was off, the nurse had to gently turn me onto my side to be able to cut the entangled hair and assess the wound.

Dad helped her hold me in place, but even though he tried his hardest to breathe through the corner of his mouth, he found himself retching. Poor dad. He'd worked in an abattoir when he was much younger but said the putrid stink of my head was even worse than that.

The lesion took a long time to heal and left me with a bald patch. In 2001, I had a small procedure to fix it.

They inserted what looked like a small boob under the skin behind my ear and then every week for three months, expanded it with a saline injection to stretch and grow the skin around it. Towards the end, it felt like I had two heads, but when they'd stretched it enough, they removed the saline pocket and used the new, enlarged skin to graft over the bald patch and my hair began to grow back.

It was amazing. You'd never know the difference now and I'm forever dyeing it different colours. Most recently it's been blue – not Marge Simpson blue, just subtle navy highlights over dark brown. But when I was self-isolating, due to the spread of Covid-19, my grey roots were shocking so I ordered a silver hue and did it myself in the bathroom. It looked ace in a kind of lockdown chic fashion, but I won't be putting any hairdressers out of business, that's for sure.

After a few days of getting used to moving my head independently, we progressed to the next stage of 'project get me out of here' – an upright position.

When you've been horizontal for so long, it takes a while for the body to acclimatise to being vertical again, so the process must be taken steadily.

Very carefully, the nurses transferred me to a tilt table, where they secured my top half and legs with straps and then slowly angled it to get me into more of a standing posture.

Like most other patients who've been on the tilt table, it left me feeling very dizzy as my blood seemed to drop to my boots. We had to try it a few times over the next couple of days until I could manage it without nearly blacking out; eventually, we did it and the nurses were able to manoeuvre me into a wheelchair.

It was great finally to be out of bed and in a different position, but I didn't have the strength or dexterity to be able to push myself yet.

Being trundled around by other people was fabulous though. I was looking at things as if for the first time, from a different angle. Everything seemed to be whizzing past me so quickly. At last, I thought, I am on the move again.

But not quite. The woman who had the final say on my

transfer to the convalescence unit in Chapel Allerton was a nightmare.

She had an aura of self-importance which was beyond irritating. I can clearly remember her badly co-ordinated green skirt and purple knitted tights covered loosely by a bobbly cardigan sprinkled with dandruff from her limp, mousey hair.

She was a good few inches shorter than mum's four foot eleven and weighed down by a chip on both shoulders. We nicknamed her 'The Poisoned Dwarf' – or PD for short.

She deserved an O.B.E. for services to condescension. The worst meeting was at my bedside when she leaned in and said: 'Now then Georgina, is your name Mary?'

I knew she was trying to check my mental capacity, but that was ridiculous. I wanted to feign ignorance just for kicks, and had I not been so desperate to get out of Jimmy's, I would have done. Instead, I went through the whole rigmarole of the alphabet-tongue thing to let her know that, no, my name was not Mary.

Then she said: 'We're on Ward 24 at St James's hospital. Are we at Chapel Allerton?' I was about to start with my tongue again, but mum butted in, furious: 'She isn't actually stupid you know,' she snapped.

That went down like a ton of bricks with PD and from then on her hackles were right up. I know it was her job to make sure I'd be okay at the next stage of my rehabilitation, but she seriously needed a lesson or two in bedside manners.

At one point, I was tempted to spell out a lot more with my tongue, but when I hovered around the 'F', mum knew where I was going with it and put the alphabet away.

After a lot of box-ticking and paper shuffling, PD curtly smiled and thanked us, then bustled off. When she returned later that day, we were informed that yes, I was of sound enough mind to be able to leave Jimmy's and I could go the next day.

Suddenly, she wasn't so irritating. I was chuffed to bits and honestly couldn't believe I was getting out of there.

Mum and dad signed a ton of papers for my release and then I was prepared for transportation and i was pretty undignified. Even though I'd passed the upright position test, my knees were still bad so the nurses commandeered a hoist.

At one point they lost purchase, clanking me into a metal pole and causing shards of pain to run through my limbs, bringing tears to my eyes. Once I'd caught my breath and mum and dad had gathered up my belongings, we were up if not quite running.

Leaving the ward felt so strange. As I was wheeled along the corridors, down lifts, past signs for radiotherapy, oncology, ICU, I genuinely felt nervous.

This hospital had been my life since my near-death in August. It was a big moment, not just for me but for my family too, a physical signal that I was on the mend and heading for recovery.

I'd gleaned a bit of information about events in the outside world during my time at Jimmy's, as visitors and the TV had kept me up to date. I also had a sense of the changing seasons because I could look out of the window and knew by the clothes people wore whether it was hot or cold. But I hadn't actually been outside myself.

I hadn't felt weather in a long time. The air smelled so different, cold in my lungs for that brief moment between exiting the hospital doors and entering the patient transport vehicle. Exhaust fumes, dust, cigarette smoke and coffee made my brain tingle with the thrilling blast of forgotten familiarity.

But when the vehicle doors closed again, I was right

back to a nose full of Dettol. You'll be pleased to know, though, that this was the most uneventful journey I experienced after my initial accident.

No blue lights, no dipping in and out of consciousness, and no need to slam on the brakes for someone unexpectedly pulling in front of us.

Mum was still with me, but this time there was a reassuring absence of heart monitors and drips. We simply pootled along like Postman Pat, smiling at each other.

It felt fantastic.

We had a similar sketch with the hoist when I arrived at Chapel Allerton, but by this point I was so relieved to be out of a proper hospital and into a place of convalescence, that I could have put up with anything.

I was taken to a ward with four other people and once mum and dad had unpacked my belongings and asked a million questions, they went home.

It sounds daft because, essentially, I was still very much in a hospital environment, but it felt alien. And even though the journey had been short, I was exhausted.

Lying there, I began to take in my new surroundings and realised I was in better shape than some of my roomies.

Two were victims of strokes – one an elderly lady, but the other a girl of eighteen. According to stroke.org.uk, only about 400 people in the UK that age are affected so her odds had been worse than mine.

Then there was another woman called Josie, who was admitted following complications after an operation, and Alison, who had MS. We were a right motley crew.

My first Christmas after the accident was spent mostly in bed, surrounded by other rehab patients in the place we eventually renamed Chapel Shithole. But mum and dad did all they could to make it as normal and jolly as possible for me. The excitement didn't quite match the time when James and I were still into Santa Claus and mum and dad told us they didn't mind what time we got up on Christmas Day – just as long as it was actually December 25.

As soon as the clock struck midnight we went tearing downstairs to see if he'd been. He had. Mum and dad were so game that they got up with us and, true to their word, let us open our presents, which had quite literally been stuffed into pairs of mum's old stockings.

By 1.00am, everything was unwrapped, including the tangerine and the twenty pence pieces right at the bottom. The only hint of excitement at 1.00am on my ward this Christmas Day was a bit of light snoring and an occasional fart.

I'd only just begun to start eating some solids again and was way off feeding myself, but mum brought in a complete Christmas meal on a plate from home, which genuinely made my mouth water. It was so utterly scrumptious.

I'd almost forgotten what it was like to consume proper food after being PEG-fed for so long (that's where they bypass your mouth completely, feeding you through a tube directly into your stomach – PEG stands for Percutaneous Endoscopic Gastronomy).

I couldn't have bolted it down if I'd wanted to because I was still re-learning to chew and swallow, so mum had cut everything into tiny pieces, but the tastes and textures were out of this world. And the smell...

Just the aroma of home cooking lifted my spirits. It was a slice of normal life outside the walls of an institution, filling me with hope. Before I could start my Christmas meal though, there was a bit of a debacle to get it heated up. For health and safety reasons, the staff didn't want mum to use their microwave and couldn't see why I wouldn't want the same seasonal slop as everybody else.

I'm not sure how she managed to do it, but somehow, mum defied the odds and got my plate of food warm.

I couldn't pull a cracker at that stage, but dad brought some anyway and we all wore paper hats while I listened to them reading out rubbish jokes. They'd bought me some presents too, which they'd duly wrapped at home and then unwrapped for me on the bed. One of the gifts was some reindeer deely boppers, which they plonked on top of my Christmas hat. I must have looked a right sight.

James and his partner were now proud parents of a little boy, Brennan, he of the future driving lesson I told you about earlier. So I insisted they have their first Christmas at home, because Chapel Allerton was no place for a six-week-old baby.

Nobody mentioned *him* that day. Mum and dad didn't ask if he was coming later and I'm glad because it saved me the embarrassment of telling them that I didn't know.

As it turned out, he didn't even bob in for half an hour. That hurt. But I just put it to the back of my mind, assuming I'd told him not to bother and enjoy time at home with his family so I could rest.

I was so gullible and foolish then, but I've learned my lesson. Once I eventually parted company with him, I vowed never to let anyone walk all over me again – and so far, they haven't.

The rest of my time at Chapel Allerton was interesting. As people, I think the staff there were probably okay, but as nurses, not so much. You would ring the bell for their attention and they wouldn't always come.

One day, mum and dad were in reception and my bell was dinging and they saw the nurses ignoring it, reading their magazines. You can imagine how well that went down.

But my overriding memory of Chapel Allerton was

boredom. Hours would go by without me doing anything.It was like living in an old people's home – and I should know, I worked in one for a few months after returning from America as an au pair, before training as a paramedic.

I quite enjoyed it as a way of gaining more caring experience and most of the residents were lovely, but these places are run like clockwork, leaving little time for spontaneous stimulation.

I wasn't strong enough to hold a book or even to turn the pages when I first arrived at Chapel Allerton.

I had to ask people for a drink, couldn't take myself to the loo and was wholly reliant on help from so many people. But it gave me time to focus on learning to speak again and, within a few months, I began to formulate words and communicate at a basic level without using the tongue method.

And while I was focussing on getting my words out, *he* was preparing *his* for the looming court case.

11

•

Standing by *Him*

HIS COURT PROCEEDINGS began at Bingley Magistrates, just on the edge of the town centre.

I say 'centre', Bingley is hardly a metropolis, but it's typical of a smallish northern town. The high street has changed over the years, but it's kept all the usuals – a post office, bakery, Dave's Bargain Centre, a load of pubs and one nightclub called Porky's, known to the locals as 'The Pig Hut' or 'Squealers'. There are a couple of basic but good curry houses and Italian restaurants and even an Arts Centre, where the Bingley Talent Contest was a big deal in the late 'seventies and early 'eighties.

Most of the children who grew up in the area learned to swim at Bingley Baths, which was just at the entrance to Myrtle Park, a fantastic green space with tennis courts, bowling green, bandstand and playground.

Every year the Bingley Agricultural Show is hosted

there, bringing in the odd famous face, such as the show jumping champion Harvey Smith or BBC *Look North* news reader Peter Levy. On the whole, it's a friendly place and the nearest town to where both *he* and I grew up.

As a child I'd passed Bingley Magistrates Court hundreds of times. That plain council building was where I imagined really bad people went to get punished and I'd always try and see if I could spot a criminal going into the building. I wondered what they might have done.

Burgled a house? Robbed a bank? Killed someone?

After all, Bingley used to be a regular haunt of mass-murderer Peter Sutcliffe, the Yorkshire Ripper, who had a job in the cemetery there and often drank at The Harvester, a pub on the edge of the shopping precinct.

On the first day of *his* proceedings, dad went but mum couldn't face it. She was better off keeping me company than having to deal with all that side of things. James was still getting his head around fatherhood and keeping the family business afloat, so didn't need the added stress of watching his now former friend potentially face prison.

It was quite the eye-opener for dad. He's just a normal law-abiding bloke, so to be stood waiting to go into a courtroom with people he'd usually avoid, was a shock.

He said most of them seemed like they hated the world. One guy did a runner from reception when he realised the police wanted him for more than one crime.

The defendants were scruffy, tired, unkempt and a few were regulars, known to the police; all of which made dad stick out like a sore thumb, all suited and booted, smelling of his usual Jean Paul Gaultier aftershave.

Luckily, the police knew dad's situation, so were kind enough to move him away from the melee until everyone had to file in. It was all very quiet and serious, you could have cut the atmosphere with a knife. The court was a small one and functionally decorated, with plain seating and fixed wooden desks at the front. Dull lighting from overhead strip lights made for a dingey atmosphere. If there'd been gorgeous sunlight outside, you'd never have known. It felt heavy.

Dad took a seat where he could get the best view of *him*. Once everyone was settled you could hear people breathing, waiting for proceedings to begin.

Dad was so churned up. How could you really forgive someone who'd nearly killed your daughter? But though he was in bits inside, his demeanour was the perfect picture of cool, calm and collected. To the point of scary.

He knew that the only way he could get to *him* was psychologically, so he just stared the whole time. Not at the court officials, not at the paperwork in front of him, just straight at *him*, dead behind the eyes.

I've since learned that dad's tactics worked – and that *he* was petrified. It was an extra layer of stress for someone who was already panic-stricken about the prospect of a custodial sentence.

In fairness, dad might have taken the staring thing a bit far because, at one point, his solicitor said to the magistrate: 'I have to bring it to your attention that the father of Georgina Hurst is in court and is intimidating my client. He won't stop staring at him.'

But the magistrate said, 'Well, he'll just have to live with it.'

It was *his* first appearance in court and the magistrate asked for his name, address and date of birth. He answered, head bowed, avoiding dad's gaze.

A date was set for a hearing and the court dispersed. There was so much evidence they needed time to go away and look at everything properly.

Unbroken

There were witness statements from Angie, Anne, his friends and the lady in the other car to sift through, police statements, photographs from the scenes of the accident, and medical documents to scour.

Much consideration had to be given to the fact that even though I was alive, I could very easily not have made it. He was a whisker away from a manslaughter charge.

Although dad wanted to make him as uncomfortable as possible, I was still besotted and honestly didn't want the man I loved to go to prison. I couldn't bear the thought of him suffering any more than he already was doing. He hadn't meant to hurt me. I knew it was an accident.

While I was still bedridden and largely speechless, I worried myself even sicker. I just kept turning scenarios over in my head about how he would cope in jail.

What if the other inmates set upon him? You hear these awful stories of men being stabbed with whittled down toothbrushes, attacked in the showers, dragged into dealing drugs and recruited into a life of crime once they are released.

I imagined having to visit him, being searched myself for drugs, unable to get out of a wheelchair to stand up and give him a hug to comfort him. It was torturous having all this going around in my head, on top of coping with my injuries. It did bring me down for a while.

I really had to try hard not to let everything get on top of me. At the same time, I didn't feel like I could share how I felt with anyone.

I knew there'd be little sympathy for him from any of my friends and family and those looking on would only assume I'd completely lost the plot. How strange that I wanted to be by his side, supporting him in court.

At that point, I wasn't cross with *him* for what he'd done to me physically, I was upset that what he'd done could mean we would have to spend more time apart. I'm glad I didn't know until much, much later that dad had been approached by people offering to take revenge.

You just don't think this happens in real life, do you? It's like something out of a film. All very shady. But it would seem it's not actually so pricey to have somebody knee-capped. Even cheaper just to put the frighteners on an enemy.

Obviously, dad didn't take them up on the offer but, now, I wouldn't blame him if he'd enjoyed imagining such scenarios. He must have died a thousand times in dad's head, probably very painfully.

For a while though, we were all in limbo. I wasn't getting any worse at Chapel Allerton, but my recovery was so slow.

He visited me from time to time, but wouldn't really have much to say. My speech therapist came and we'd try and get the muscles in my mouth and lips moving again.

James and Brennan kept popping in and I noticed how much the baby had grown. Time was marching on in the outside world and I wasn't moving anywhere.

To take my mind off the impending sentence, I used my time-travel trick again, mentally transporting myself back to happier moments in my life.

When the young girl on my ward with MS had an American visitor one day, her accent reminded me of living as an au pair in Virginia. The couple I lived with in the Aquia Harbour gated community were called Eric and Susan. They were a bit weird, but their children were fine, considering.

Whenever off-duty, I made a point of finding things to do away from the house, to give us all a bit of space.

Aquia Harbour had their own medical rescue station at the gates as you went in. The head of the unit had a really unfortunate name – Doyle Fuchs – but when I approached him to see if I could help out at all, he was brilliant and got me on an Emergency Medical Training course for one night a week over three months. I loved it and it wasn't long before I was promoted from just observing to actually being useful.

Remembering one case made me guffaw out loud on the ward. I'd forgotten all about it. We received a call out to what can only be described as an 'amorous couple'. They'd obviously been having a bit of afternoon delight and somehow, during the course – or should I say intercourse – of proceedings, she had gone into some kind of spasm and trapped him inside of her.

I don't know how long they'd been trying to separate from each other, but when we went to find them it was very tricky trying to keep a straight face.

We pulled up at their bungalow and gingerly let ourselves in, calling as we did so, assuming they'd be in the bedroom. But no. They'd had to make their way to the telephone in the lounge – together, which is where we found him on top. They were mortified.

We covered them with blankets as best we could to protect their modesty and, between blushes, managed to manoeuvre them into the back of the ambulance to drive them to the hospital. But guess who got the job of sitting in the back with them? Muggins here. Luckily, they weren't in any pain, but it fell on me to make small talk: 'Sooooo, do you come here often?'

When we eventually got to the hospital, they gave the lady a relaxant injection and he managed to break free. It's quite common, apparently, but I've never heard of a case like it since.

I wonder what methods of separation they'd exhausted before calling an ambulance. Ice packs to cool things down? Olive oil to loosen things up? The mind boggles.

I'd been in America about five months when mum came over for a visit, but as I waited to collect her in arrivals, she didn't recognise me as I'd put on so much weight. She just walked straight past. I let her carry on for a while and then she turned around and I was like: 'Hello, it's me!'

It's not surprising I'd put a pound or ten on, because there seemed to be a fast food outlet on every street corner. England hadn't yet been flooded with all things American at that stage. Drive-thru was practically unheard of in Bradford in the 1990s.

I love America and could imagine myself living there in the future. The people are lovely and, in practical terms, it's a fantastic place for wheelchair users. The only thing I can't believe when I visit now is the amount of people who use mobility scooters unnecessarily.

I've been to a shopping mall with friends and carers and always hired an electric scooter – mainly because it's easier to talk to each other when you're side by side, rather than having someone push you from behind. But the amount of times we've got to the entrance of a shop and the assistant has said: 'Just park it there and walk in.'

When I say I can't walk they are flabbergasted: 'What do you mean you can't walk?' And I have to say: 'I'm not in this for the good of my health.' They trip over themselves to help once they know you are a real-life disabled person.

The people I met on the EMT course in Virginia were really welcoming and I made some great friends, with the same sense of humour as me. My favourite person was my tutor, a woman called Lori. She came to my rescue and let me stay with her when the family I was working for threw me out after nine months.

It had all come to a head when Eric and Susan noticed that I'd become friends with another au pair called Rachel.

Unbroken

Rachel lived with a neighbouring family on the same estate, so we got talking at the park initially and then used to arrange to meet up, so the children could play together.

That was against Eric and Susan's rules because they didn't want their children mixing with others in case they caught germs, but I thought it was important for them to have friends outside of the family setting.

Anyway, one afternoon Rachel was at my place with her two, and Eric and Susan came home early. The neighbours had obviously been spying and tipped them off. They told me to leave immediately.

The problem was, I still had three months left on my working visa and desperately didn't want my American adventure to end. So Rachel's family very kindly took me in for a couple of weeks, and then I went home for a short visit while Lori came up with a perfect plan.

When I returned to America, I lived with Lori and worked part-time as her au pair and part-time volunteering for the EMT. My first job in her house was hilarious – she had me dressed up as Barney the Dinosaur for her daughter's birthday party. The things you do.

And in fact it was during those interim weeks in Yorkshire that I first got together with *him*, at the Brown Cow pub in Bingley, on a Friday night just before closing time.

He was stood in a small corridor section between the door and the main room and I thought he was gorgeous.

I'd already earmarked him as 'Mr Potential' when my friends and I used to walk behind him and his friends on the way to the bus stop after school, ker-chings at the ready.

There was just something about his cheeky swagger and scruffy school blazer I really fancied. Even though he was in the year below me, he seemed mature back then, his friends a bit tough, full of confidence.

Occasionally, I'd catch a glimpse of him walking between lessons or – joy of joys – in his PE kit on the rugby pitch, but would never dare approach him directly.

I hadn't seen him properly since leaving school. He was a friend of my brother, but James tended to go out more than have people back to the house, and because I'd been away at college in Stafford and then working in the US, I'd not bumped into him. So, full of the Dutch courage that only last orders can bring, I took a deep breath, walked straight up and started snogging him.

Just like that.

There was no resistance on his part. His mates couldn't believe it, but whooped and cheered, giving it the: 'Oi, Oi, I think you're in there,' while I just melted into him.

He was a great kisser, I'll give him that. I went all-out, running my fingers through the back of his hair as he pressed his firm body into mine, swaying slightly with the booze and bustle around us. It felt like fate, as if the incident in Virginia had happened specifically to lead me to this moment, to him, and I knew I didn't want to let him go.

Over the next couple of weeks things progressed rapidly on the physical front, snatching moments whenever and wherever we could, to do what most twenty-somethings do in that first rush of love. I spent as much time with him as I could and by the time I was due to fly back to America, I knew I'd fallen hook, line and sinker.

We promised to write to each other – airmail letters, which seem so quaint now. I wrote to him every week and couldn't wait to get his missives back.

He wrote about three all together and they were never full of love and longing, more along the lines of: 'Had a great night in Bingley. Got mortalled.'

I just thought he was a typical bloke and told myself I

101

wasn't into that soppy stuff anyway. Plus, back in the States, it was full-on because Lori had also arranged for me to have a week in the trauma unit in Washington DC.

I'd never seen anything like it. Nearly every trauma was a gunshot wound. The doctors would perform surgery there and then. Patients came in with head shots, heart shots, shots that just missed vital organs, shattered ankles, the lot. It was so intense.

A lot of it was gangland based but, strangely, I didn't feel scared. I just saw vulnerable people in need of help.

In a situation like that, it doesn't matter how or why someone is injured, they just need to be stitched back up. Perhaps I've always been able to mentally distance myself from the terror of a situation.

I dread to think how some of these people paid their medical bills afterwards. Say what you want about the NHS, but if you're ever in a life and death situation in the UK, at least you don't have the added pressure of wondering how you will foot the bill once you are well again.

And long may that last.

12

•

Can't See the Wood for the Trees

IN APRIL 1999, *he* was given a custodial sentence of six months for Dangerous Driving. It was reduced to three and he was banned from driving for a year.

He did a week in Armley jail – HMP Leeds – and was then moved to North Sea Camp Prison in Lincolnshire where, according to dad, they pick cucumbers and watch TV all day. It's an open one, like Jeffrey Archer ended up in when found guilty of perjury and perverting the course of justice in 2001.

But six weeks after his initial sentence, *he* was released with a tag. He still thinks his sentence was harsh and reckons his solicitor didn't tell the full story. Whatever.

James jokingly suggested to dad that the pair of them should have captured him and locked him in a shed, so he missed his tag curfew.

On hearing what he'd got I was distraught. All I could think about was him being taken away to Armley in a police van. My panic was immense. I couldn't imagine what he must have been feeling at the time. Mum and dad were glad that justice had been done but they, along with James, felt the sentence was woeful.

I lost my appetite completely. I couldn't eat or drink and nothing stayed down when I tried. It got to the stage where the doctors were very worried and began trying to get lines into me for rehydration. But my veins were so narrow they had to try in my feet and even my groin in the end.

Six days after *he* had gone into prison, a nurse at Chapel Allerton rang 999 because my blood pressure had dropped down to fifty over forty.

I was rushed to Leeds General Infirmary and mum and dad were woken up by another phone call in the middle of the night telling them to get to hospital as soon as they could. I had developed pneumonia, septicaemia and a pulmonary embolism. It could have been a coincidence, but I sometimes wonder if I hadn't been so weak with worry, would I have ended up so physically wiped out? We'll never know. It was a particularly low point of the whole debacle.

He said his feelings of terror being driven away from court in the police van were overridden by sadness, because he knew he wouldn't be able to see me every day. He claimed the worst punishment was being apart from me. And I believed him. He was put on suicide watch in Armley, but I don't think he was suicidal at all. I think he pretended to be on the edge so he'd be treated more leniently. He told me he'd been sharing a cell with a murderer for the first few nights and then when news got to him that my health had spiralled so rapidly, he couldn't hack it anymore.

He got moved to the hospital wing of the jail, where he was closely monitored and away from other inmates.

But guess what? And this should have been another big

red flag to tell me that he wasn't husband material – he met someone in jail he knew! Honestly.

It was someone he'd grown up with, who was now apparently looking out for him on the inside. What were the chances? It showed the circles he moved in.

He said the prison officers were really good to him in jail and let him call the hospital three times a day to check up on my progress. I was in and out of consciousness, so don't remember much of that, but the nurses were kind enough to update him on my progress.

It all had to be done with phone cards from prison back then, and he was only allowed a certain amount of time to talk. So as soon as the nurses knew it was him calling, they'd answer as quickly as they could to save him credit.

He told me that when he was in Armley prison, a 'smackhead' tried to steal his phonecards. But the guy who was minding his back got the situation sorted.

I can't believe I was actually going to marry him. Imagine what our wedding reception would have been like? Half of West Yorkshire's underworld could have rocked up for a buffet and a bust-up.

The day he was released on a tag, he came to see me in Chapel Allerton. I was so happy. He'd got the train to Leeds and then a bus straight up, only stopping for a can of Coke on the way. He had a suit on because that's what he'd worn to court, so it was the outfit they'd kept hold of until he was allowed back on the streets.

He looked a bit thinner and pale and had grown a goatee beard. I hated that goatee, but at the time couldn't care less because I'd missed him so much. He just walked straight towards me, staring and smiling, leaned over and gave me a massive kiss: 'I'm out,' he said.

I was so utterly relieved his sentence was over. It wasn't

ideal that he had a tag on his ankle, but as long as he stuck to the curfew, he would be fine. He was free.

He told me a bit about what it was like in both prisons – the food, the people, what there was to do, how he kept himself to himself as best he could.

He said at times it was scary knowing there was no escape. It sounded awful and we agreed that prison wasn't dissimilar to hospital in many ways. But at least he had free time, where he could leave his cell and walk around.

I still couldn't talk much at that point and was a long way off walking, but I was more interested in hearing his voice and seeing his face than wallowing in my situation.

I just wanted him there to hold my hand after what seemed like an age. I felt my whole body relax. I hadn't realised how much tension had manifested itself inside every part of me. It was like I'd been holding my breath for six weeks and now, finally, I could let go.

He could have stayed much longer with me in Chapel Allerton that day, but chose not to. Instead, he got the bus back to the village where he was living and 'bumped into' his mate Jay, who persuaded him to go for a pint to celebrate his release. If it hadn't been for his mum ringing him again and again, he would have missed his curfew and been straight back to prison.

After everything he'd been through, he still couldn't take responsibility for himself. And his priorities hadn't changed. He still wanted to spend more time with his mates than with me.

Rumours were rife about his unfaithfulness after he was released from prison. Bingley has a lot of eyes.

I genuinely can't remember if anyone explicitly tried to tell me what he was up to but, in all honesty, if they had, I wouldn't have believed them – or rather, would have chosen not to believe them. It's hard to imagine now how much I felt for him at the time. Even harder to believe that in the September of that year, I agreed to move in with him.

13

•

Brotherly Love

I FELT MANY CONFLICTING emotions during my time in Chapel Allerton. Anger at being in this situation, helplessness because all I could do was try my hardest to get better, and an overriding sense of gratitude that friends and family were going above and beyond to brighten me up and cheer me on.

I was rarely embarrassed because my dignity had gone out of the window long since. Months of being given bed baths by all manner of men and women can do that to you.

I regularly had someone sticking a finger up my bum to help me empty my bowels. It doesn't get more undignified than that, but we tried to make light of it as best we could.

One nurse was great. Every time she proffered a digit, we pretended I'd given birth to a baby poo and named each 'child'. Poo-cinda. Dung-can. Sue-age.

I was so hairy too.

The hair on my head had got thinner with the trauma,

but honestly, you could have put rollers in the hairs on my legs. It was just my body's way of coping, plus the massive doses of steroids. My eyelashes were so long they touched the top of my eyebrows.

You'd think that with everything else going on, the last thing I'd be fussed about was hairy legs. But for some reason, it did matter to me.

Mum had offered to shave them as soon as was medically possible but, in the end, there was no need because as my body recovered, the steroids were reduced and my leg hairs just fell out.

Even though we'd had various issues with the nursing staff at Chapel Allerton, you couldn't fault the physiotherapy and occupational therapy centre there.

Not just because it was boredom-busting (the hours dragged between sessions), but if I hadn't had all that help and encouragement to get parts of my body moving as soon as I could, then there's no way I would have been able to cycle across Europe and eventually pole dance.

I really surprised myself with what I achieved there. Woodwork – or Craft Design and Technology as it was called at Bingley Grammar circa 1988 – was never really my forte.

I think I got about as far as making a key ring and possibly a teapot stand at school. But at Chapel Allerton, the projects were much more ambitious. With a lot of help I rustled up a bird table, wheelbarrow and a rocking chair.

My hand movements weren't great at all, but the occupational therapists guided and steadied me. I don't think anybody would have felt safe if I'd been let loose with a chisel or two-speed hammer drill on my own.

But it wasn't just about improving my physicality as much as I could, I wanted to be able to produce something to give to my loved ones, to say thank you.

Unbroken

Mum never wanted thanks, she was just thrilled that I could move my hands. But she had a bit of tunnel vision at this stage and was always looking for the next goal, the next milestone I could reach.

Her belief that I would continue to improve never wavered. That's one of the main reasons I keep doing what I'm doing now. Mum instilled that drive in me constantly to only look forward and challenge myself.

These occupational therapists are very clever. At the time, you think you're just focussing on the task in hand, but quite often, you start talking about other things, opening up.

It just sort of happens. Though how on earth they understood me at that stage, with the all the background noise of carpentry going on over my bird-like voice, I'll never know.

Somehow they gently coaxed me into producing a rocking chair for my nephew, which had Brennan's name on the back of it, as well as a wheelbarrow for mum and dad and a bird table for *him*. I've no idea what happened to the chair and the wheelbarrow, but I'm pretty sure *he* won't have kept hold of the bird table.

In that sense, I got a lot out of Chapel Allerton, but I still didn't think the actual nursing care was that great. Slipshod, I think mum called it. Severely lacking, dad said. From X-rays and paperwork mysteriously disappearing to an untreated infection landing me in Leeds General Infirmary – again – it was all unnecessary drama and stress.

For weeks, I'd had blood in my wee. Mum flagged it up numerous times, but they fobbed it off as menstruation gone awry as my body 'settled down'.

Mum eventually lost it and said: 'Can you name me any other woman in the world who has had a period for nearly four weeks running? It can't possibly be.'

Lo and behold, two nights later I was rushed to the LGI with my blood pressure dangerously low. A urinary tract infection had taken hold and I had to be flushed with drips full of antibiotics and monitored closely.

My brother James freaked out when he came to visit me in hospital after that incident. He said that I looked like I had serious brain damage, because I was sloped to one side and dribbling.

As if he hadn't got enough on his plate with a baby and keeping a business afloat, his road rage continued to bubble away too. It was like he was looking for anyone to make the slightest mistake so he could beep his horn, flash his lights and shout: 'Bloody idiot. My sister's in a wheelchair because of people like you.'

I know James is proud of what I've achieved since the crash and he was a big fan before it. He likes to tell the tale of when I came home from Liverpool for the weekend after qualifying as a paramedic.

I went to see him at work in my uniform and he was welling up. Then we walked into Bingley together and apparently lots of men were sounding their car horns and he said: 'Well, they're not bloody well beeping at me, are they George?'

Remembering moments like that are hard for James because it makes him miss the 'old' me.

I was his big sister who built sandcastles with him on holidays, stuck her tongue out across the tea table when dad wasn't looking and squashed on the sofa with him to watch *Rentaghost* after school.

I was who he was forced to watch perform a rendition of 'Itsy Bitsy Teenie Weenie Yellow Polkadot Bikini' at a ballet show in Bradford, who'd fought with him over the best seat in the car, the final can of cider in the fridge or the last sausage on the plate (before my brief vegetarian phase, which ended when I realised I didn't like vegetables).

But he needn't be sad, we've got some great memories from our childhood and lots of time to create many more.

In a way, it's better now because growing up we were just your standard siblings, falling out and taking each other for granted. I don't take James for granted one bit now and I know we'll support each other whatever paths our lives take.

One thing neither of us could have anticipated though was the amount of media attention I would receive following the accident.

I've been in numerous papers, on local television and part of a series on BBC Radio 5 Live. At the time of the crash, it was front page news in our local rag.

At various points in my recovery, the media have caught up with my progress. I was featured in a magazine at my brother's first wedding because I was a bridesmaid and insistent I'd be able to walk down the aisle (which I did).

But while I was in Chapel Allerton, it was *him* who courted the press with a story about his car being stolen while he was visiting me. Looking back, I can't believe he hadn't been banned from driving straight after the crash, but I suppose you have to let justice run its course.

Anyway, he'd arrived at the convalescence centre as usual, parking in the main car park. He locked the doors but accidentally left his new mobile inside.

During the time of his short visit, someone had nicked the vehicle. *He* took that personally: 'Nothing's going right anymore. Why me?,' he said.

After reporting it to the police, he decided to use his friend's mobile to text his own phone to say 'please can I have my car back, no questions asked, because I need it to visit my seriously ill fiancée in hospital'.

He must have laid his sob story on very thick because within days his car was returned to the exact same spot.

Somehow, the press got wind of this and decided it was worth a few columns. But it really riled my family because the tone of the article was all sympathy for him.

He'd failed to mention the reason why I was in hospital in the first place. Dad was tempted to write to the paper and tell them the whole story, but he didn't have the energy.

He wasn't going to waste a minute more of his time thinking about *him*.

14

•

A Whole New Chapter

I STAYED AT Chapel Allerton until the end of May 1999. I was past the critical stage but absolutely nowhere near fixed and couldn't wait to get out – especially as *he* was now at large again, albeit with his tag still on.

Mum and dad set up a mini-home for me in their lounge, to give me a bit of independence. They enlisted the help of ICU nurse-cum-interior-designer Lou, and between them made it both practical and pretty.

It had a bed, table and chairs, TV, everything I needed. At that point I still spent most of my time sat up in a bed, but I could be manoeuvred into a wheelchair to get me from place to place. My knees were on the mend at least.

Carers were there 24/7. They were obviously medically trained, but much of what they did was general care.

Although I could eat solid food, I still couldn't feed myself. Neither could I go to the toilet or have a shower independently; but at least I could choose when to do those things, rather than be part of some wider, institutionalised routine.

You could have set your clock by the way my life was timetabled at Chapel Allerton. One thing I was adamant about was making sure mum and dad didn't have to do the bathing and feeding etc. It was important to me that they didn't think I saw them as home-help.

He visited me at mum and dad's house, but hated it. Dad tried his utmost to be civil, but it must have been through gritted teeth. Mum had no hate, she just got on with it, hoping that I would eventually see the light.

During this time, he was supposed to be looking for a suitable place for us to live together. He had some savings from before the accident and his boss had been good enough to keep his plumbing job open for him for when he got out of prison, so he wasn't penniless.

My final compensation hadn't been sorted out by this time, but he knew that all the costs for my care were being met through his insurance company. And thank God he had been insured because I really don't know what would have happened otherwise.

He split his time between work, trawling estate agents, visiting me at mum and dad's and going out with his friends in Bingley.

Still banned from driving, he had to get everywhere on a bicycle, bus or by blagging a lift. I didn't mind him going out with his mates. It's not like I could have joined him and I didn't want to hold him back. But while I was being the martyr, insisting he enjoyed himself, he didn't stop at having fun with just his pals.

I don't know any names – it might have only been one girl – but it seems his heart was never really with me.

Unbroken

My friends still visited and James regularly bobbed round with Brennan, who was now weaning. I didn't realise, but James particularly struggled with visits at mealtimes. He hated the fact that I was at the same level of being able to feed myself as his baby. He knew that soon, Brennan would be doing more with his body than I could, and the comparison really upset him. He felt it was so unfair.

I'd planned to be chief babysitter for my nephew, the proud auntie pushing him in his stroller around Myrtle Park, treating him to an ice cream, watching him take his first steps. In all likelihood, James thought, Brennan would probably end up pushing me.

There was still a lot of work to do on my physicality, so when I moved home after Chapel Allerton, I spent three days a week in Skipton at a Young Disabled Centre.

'Young,' my backside.

The next age up from myself can't have been less than fifty. It was about occupational health and wellbeing, getting you moving and used to the outside world again. A great idea in theory.

Every day I was collected by a transport ambulance and taken there with my carer. But after a while, I was told I couldn't bring a carer anymore because she was surplus to requirements. The centre wanted me to rely on staff already in the building. This was a real blow to me, because I knew they wouldn't be as good.

The next day, mum turned up instead and did all that my carer would have done. Unfortunately, the boss twigged what was happening and banned mum too. It wasn't long before we gave that place up as a bad job – and I didn't miss it one bit.

I didn't like the ambience. It felt like I'd been lumped in with a lot of people who weren't like me. Some had solely physical disabilities, but others clearly had cognitive issues too – either they'd been born that way or had developed them following an accident or stroke.

I would look around and think 'get me out of here'. In a way, that was probably a good sign, because it meant that I hadn't given up, that I knew I didn't want to spend the rest of my life being stuck in a room and dependent.

Mealtimes were soul destroying. It was a community lunch where we were all wheeled in and seated at a table together without even getting to choose where we sat.

We were encouraged to feed ourselves as much as we could, but just looking around at the other diners was so depressing. Some of us wore bibs and others clearly had no chance of ever being able to get a spoon to their mouth independently again.

The fayre was far from gourmet because most of it was soft, as nobody could cut it up. I wanted to be at a table with family or friends – or just at home, where there was a sense of normality.

And because some of the people there weren't fully functioning mentally, the healthcare assistants seemed to take the attitude that we were all a nugget short of a happy meal. It was easier for them to adopt the same patronising voice towards everyone than look at and treat us as individuals.

More often than not, they would talk across us, to each other, and not really engage with the task at hand.

It was particularly frustrating for me because I knew what they were doing, but due to the fact that I still couldn't speak clearly at this point, they treated me like I was retarded.

There was one particularly horrible time when a healthcare assistant was setting me up at a table and turned to her colleague. 'How many more inmates are left to come through?' she said. It was really humiliating.

Unbroken

I'll never forget her face. She was young, dressed in white and had short blonde hair. She was in completely the wrong job, which I managed to convey to her through various means of communication. I think an 'uncontrollable kick' might have come into it. She didn't do it again.

Once, I was let out into the real world to try an everyday task. They decided it would be a good idea for me to go shopping for some pasta and then make a meal with it.

I was carted to a supermarket in Skipton in the patient transport van and manhandled onto a mobility scooter.

The scooter was massive – so cumbersome. I hadn't even had chance to practise using it elsewhere, so it was a complete nightmare to manoeuvre.

And at the shop, most of the ingredients I needed were too high for me to see, never mind reach. I was followed everywhere by the healthcare assistant, who just kept picking stuff of the shelf and saying: 'Is this the pasta you want?' or 'Can you reach out and get the sauce from the third shelf? Go on, you can do it.'

Paying at the till was just as excruciating.

'Have you got your purse, Georgina? Can you count the right money out?'

I was being treated like a primary school pupil. They just didn't get that, mentally, I was absolutely fine.

When we returned to the centre and unloaded the ingredients on the counter in the specially adapted kitchen, things didn't get much better.

It was all: 'How much pasta do you think you'll need?' And: 'Once the pasta is in the pan, what do we do then?'

The thing is, they hadn't even asked me if I liked pasta from the outset. For the record, I do, but they didn't know that. I can cook very well for myself now, no thanks to them.

But there was light at the end of the tunnel because

*Growing up
in Cottingley*

Happy in my teenage years

My time as an au pair and EMT (emergency medical technician) in the USA

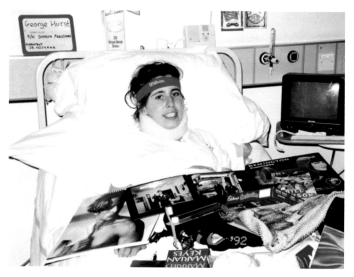

*My rehab starts at
Chapel Allerton
hospital*

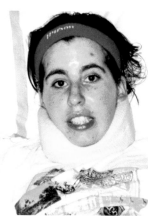

Christmas 1998, a bit different to normal and my fist visit home

Showing my appreciation to the Emergency Services that attended the accident

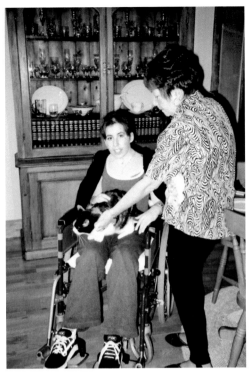

*Me, mum and
Minty the cat*

*Mum and Dad
finally get out for
New Year's Eve*

*Christmas dinner
at home at last*

I finally get to meet my nephew, above, who was born in the early days of my rehab journey

while I'd been going through the motions of making tuna pasta bake, *he* had finally found a bungalow for us, so patient transport services would have a new address to collect me from.

Nobody could understand why I still wanted to spend the rest of my life with him. But I was honestly, genuinely excited. It just felt like a whole new chapter was starting in our lives.

15

•

Together Alone

MUM SWORE THAT if I moved in with *him*, she would never come to visit. I didn't believe her at first, thought she was bluffing, but she wasn't.

She also said the house he'd chosen was in a rough area and could see from the estate agent's details that it was completely unsuitable for my needs. Turns out she was right about that. But I didn't care then, it was a home for my fiancé and me. He'd stepped up and found a place where we could be together. When we got the keys to the bungalow, he said he wanted to seal the deal by carrying me over the threshold, which I thought was so cute.

That day in September when he was due to collect me from mum and dad's, I was full of hope. My belongings had been packed by one of my carers, I was dressed and ready to go and sat in my wheelchair by the window thinking this was going to be such a perfect day.

The sun was making a concerted effort to shine through the drizzle, catching the odd leaf fluttering to the grass. To the west, I saw the beginning of a rainbow and it felt like a sign that everything was going to work out alright.

The doorbell rang and I could hear dad go to open it and begin talking to him. Mum joined them both and even though I couldn't make out what they were saying, I could tell mum's voice was clipped and dad's had a note of warning in it.

I understand now that they had my best interests at heart, but at the time it felt like they were barring him from my room, laying the ground rules about how to treat their daughter.

I was cross that they were so clingy and couldn't see that I just wanted to get my life back on track. I didn't want to be stuck living in my parents' lounge in my twenties.

My physical needs involved a hell of a lot of paperwork and so, as well as my personal belongings, there were various files which needed to come too.

Some were medical details in terms of which tablets I needed to take at what time, along with telephone numbers and records of my care to date. Another folder was full of logging forms for the carers, like handover notes and time sheets. I think mum and dad were pressing home the point that if I was living with him, he had to pick up the reins.

As he opened the door to my room, I thought he looked a bit ashen. He'd been out the night before to mark his last night of bachelorhood, so had a hangover. But he did his best to smile and dangled the house keys from his right index finger and said: 'Let's go.' The taxi waited patiently outside as he loaded the few bags I had into the boot, making sure to leave enough space for my wheelchair.

While he busied himself with that, mum and dad both

gave me a hug. There was nothing left to say that hadn't already been said about this situation.

I knew they didn't want me to go – there was no secret there – but I did respect the fact that they were letting me get on with it.

When he tried to reassure mum by telling her he'd look after me, mum just said: 'Yeah, you make sure you do.'

There were no tears from my parents, just a stiff upper lip resignation that their daughter was being wheeled away from them by a boy who had nearly killed her.

They didn't help him help me into the taxi. They just waved and closed the door. But I was looking forwards now, not back and didn't want to see them stood there anyway.

He pushed my chair down the driveway and stopped outside the front passenger seat, angling it into a position so that he could help lift me in. I still hadn't regained much strength – let alone flexibility – by this point, so it wasn't just a case of getting me in and leaving me to make myself comfortable. He had to ensure I was sat straight and my seat-belt was on correctly. It was like he was scared to touch me in case he broke me again, so the whole scenario took forever.

Once he'd buckled me in, he hefted my chair into the boot and took his place in the back seat, giving the driver directions.

The journey took less time than it had to get me into the car in the first place. I couldn't turn around properly to see his face as we drove, so I spent most of the time staring out of the window, watching the rest of the world go by, wondering where this next chapter would take us.

When we pulled up outside our bungalow on the edge of a council estate near Bingley, I felt things were finally falling into place for us.

We'd endured such a journey to get to this day and now

we could start our lives again. I'd obviously forgiven him for the accident, and he'd stood by me all this time in hospital.

He'd survived prison, I'd got through hospital and after more than a year of being in separate places, we at last had a space to call our own.

He paid the driver, then rescued the wheelchair out of the boot, dumping it onto the pavement, still folded. He then grabbed my bags and carried them to the front of the house before returning to the chair. After a bit of faffing and a lot of swearing, he unfolded it, locked it into position and wheeled it around to my passenger door.

Leaning over me, he unclipped my seatbelt and asked: 'Ready?' 'Ready,' I replied, and he did his best to scoop me out of the seat and into the wheelchair.

I was in a bit of a slump, but didn't want to ruin the moment by asking him to start adjusting me. I knew we'd be at our front door in no time.

We thanked the driver and *he* began to push me up the path. When we reached the door, he put the brakes on, fumbled for the keys in his pocket and unlocked it. He placed my luggage inside, then turned around and walked back towards me. Even before the accident, he'd never fully picked me up, so it felt strange when he reached down and tried to scoop me into his arms.

I could tell he was worried that he might hurt me, but I encouraged him to continue. With his left arm under my legs and his right under my armpits, he awkwardly gathered me up. I wanted to put my arms around his shoulders and cling to his neck, but my upper body was still very weak, so I just moved them as near as I could.

Then, with a 1-2-3-hup, he carried me through the door and into the lounge, where he then plonked me on the sofa. Not exactly gently, but I felt his heart was in the right place.

Next, he propped me up with cushions and went back to collect my chair. I could hear him clanking it across the lip of the doorway and into the little entrance hall, where he left it and headed straight to the kitchen fridge to collect a couple of beers for us to celebrate.

'Cheers,' he said as he entered and pulled the ring of one of the cans, handing it to me. 'Cheers,' I replied, wondering how he could have already forgotten that I wasn't meant to drink while I was still on medication.

He pulled the ring of his own can and took a long slurp. I just held mine as best I could on my knee and tried to remember the last time I'd actually been drunk.

We had about an hour on our own, and in that time, he got me back into my wheelchair and gave me the grand tour.

The house wasn't adapted in any way for a person with my needs. The doors weren't very wide, the carpet was hard to wheel over, the kitchen was the perfect height for someone who could stand, and the bathroom was devoid of grab rails.

The décor was okay, but not really my style. It was a bit plain and dated. I just assumed that eventually we'd go shopping together and choose some nice fixtures and fittings. It was a goal I mentally set myself there and then – to be like a normal couple, out buying normal things for our home.

I still needed twenty-four-hour help, so after that rare hour together, one of my carers came for her first shift in our new home. He cancelled the overnight staff for good, saying he would be perfectly capable of looking after me if any problems arose in the night.

We soon established a little routine and I have to say that the initial month of cohabitation was great. I didn't even mind going to the Young Disabled Centre because I knew I was going home to him at the end of the day.

He would cycle off to work at 7.00am and I'd either be

taken to Skipton or work on my speech or body at home with the carers. Everything I did took ages, so by the time I'd had breakfast and then been showered and dressed, we would be thinking about lunch. The day soon passed.

Occasionally dad came to see me, but never mum. Or dad would collect me and take me to their house.

The happy time with him didn't last long. From late-October onwards it was starting to become clear that he really didn't want to be in this situation with me anymore.

He coped by drinking, the amount of which crept up and up. He'd start by having a can of lager on a night in front of the TV, then it would be two, then three and it wasn't long before he was coming back from work every night with at least a four pack. I could understand that he needed to relax after a day at work, but he shouldn't have been getting drunk. I felt he was trying to block me out.

We couldn't really socialise either, because his driving ban hadn't been lifted yet and I still needed a lot of care.

Pubs were out of the question, not only in terms of practicality, but also because my speech was so bad that I wouldn't have been able to join in the conversation.

And, lets face it, if I had been able to go to the pub, the last thing his close friends would've wanted was a physical reminder of the part they'd played in my condition. After all, they were the ones who had encouraged him to race to McDonalds the previous summer.

It soon became all about *him*. He said some of the carers were turning against him and I can see why.

They must have looked at me and my needs, then at him and thought, 'What is this guy bringing to the table?' But instead of stepping up, sacking off the beer and mucking in, he decided to think that everybody hated him. He began to go to the pub with his friends, leaving me behind.

He told anyone who'd listen how much he did for me, but the reality was very different. Even when he was at home, the carers still showered and dressed me, helped me at mealtimes, assisted with the bathroom and so on.

He claimed to have cooked tea for us every night, but that was utter nonsense – the carers did it. *He* couldn't even cook an omelette.

I felt he was beginning to resent having to push me around the house in the wheelchair, but my arms simply weren't strong enough at that point for me to be able to propel myself anywhere.

It became a nightmare. We were both living the reality of the aftermath of a near fatal car crash, which he'd caused. We both felt trapped.

Unlike other couples who first move in together, there was absolutely nothing going on in the bedroom department either. I could have laid there and taken it, but don't think he wanted that. I think I turned him off. But I didn't want to do it either – which should have been another clanging alarm bell.

I felt no desire to get my kit off and, even if I had, he'd have probably called the carers to get me undressed.

My body just didn't seem to want his anymore. I think it was so focussed on healing that an active sex life was way down my list of priorities.

So in November, when mum and dad told me they'd been offered the use of a villa in Clearwater, Florida, and asked if I'd like to go with them, I didn't hesitate.

16

•

Reality Bites

THE VILLA HOLIDAY on Florida's Gulf Coast came about via one of dad's contacts at work. It sounded ideal, but took a lot of planning.

I'd never been on holiday in a wheelchair before and my parents had never taken anyone disabled abroad either. It was a big deal, but we managed.

It had been nearly sixteen months since the accident and this was the first time that mum, dad and I had really come up for air and tried something fun. It was a challenge, but who wouldn't want one in the Sunshine State?

Other than essentials, I didn't pack many clothes. My body shape had changed a lot since my last beach holiday and none of the shops in West Yorkshire were stocking sarongs, what with it being winter.

We decided it would be a better idea to get kitted out in America. We could go to one of the huge malls and start from scratch. Plus, with my wheelchair and mum and dad's luggage, we already had our hands full.

Because I'd been cooped up for so long, either in hospital, rehab or living with *him*, even Manchester Airport felt exciting. It was like a mini holiday in itself, seeing all the different shops, cafés and unfamiliar faces. I wanted to sniff all the perfumes in Duty Free, I was busting to try on sandals and sunglasses in Accessorise and the lure of a glass of wine in a public setting was irresistible. It was sensory overload and I loved it. I'd have been quite happy for the flight to be delayed by twenty-four hours.

The check-in and boarding process went surprisingly smoothly. That's one good thing about being disabled, priority boarding is a given so there's no hanging about in queues or double-checking the departures board every five minutes. Once you're on their radar, you just take everything in your stride and wait for them to call you. Or at least, that was my experience when I travelled accompanied. When I began flying on my own years later, I was faced with a whole host of headaches.

My breakages had healed but the wound at the back of my head from the halo still needed tending to, so we hired an American nurse out there who was fantastic. She helped with a lot of other aspects of my care too, like washing, dressing and using the bathroom. She was just the right balance of helpful but unobtrusive, so mum and dad could relax too.

The accommodation was beautiful, an absolutely stunning villa with fabulous views of the coast and easy access to the town and beach. Quite the contrast to my hutch-like bungalow in Bingley, which even my childhood rabbit, Black Eyes, would have felt trapped in.

But even though we were surrounded by scenery and

sunshine, I think it hit home how limiting life can be for a wheelchair user. It just wasn't set up for someone without full use of their legs. Small things to other people, but huge to me.

The windows, for example, were just that bit too high for me to appreciate the coastline. The doors were narrow, the shower taps tough to turn, the plug socket tricky to reach over the kitchen counter, the bed a bit difficult to wheel around. Things I would never have even thought about before the crash were suddenly a priority.

Even though we were faced with new issues daily, I really enjoyed those two weeks in Clearwater. It was such a literal and metaphorical breath of fresh air and we made the most of every minute.

We even ventured out to some of the theme parks. Obviously, rollercoasters were out of the question, but nothing was stopping me from soaking up the atmosphere.

I loved people-watching and ate a lot of hotdogs. The wide-open spaces and flat surfaces made it easy for mum and dad to push me around and we found loads of activities for people like me. We were on a mission. Team Hurst were seeking out sedentary stuff in the Sunshine State.

Mum and I enjoyed various beauty treatments, including a manicure which involved reindeers being painted onto our nails. I know, it sounds hideous, but they looked surprisingly good, really artistic and it was December. Dad was just happy to see us two happy and took himself off for a wander while mum and I were pampered.

It wasn't long before I began to start feeling a little bit like my old self again and it came as a bit of a shock to me when I realised I wasn't missing *him*.

We went to the nearby beach a couple of times, but didn't spend hours there because wheelchairs and sand aren't natural bedfellows. I just wanted to feel the warm seashore between my toes and smell the breeze. Even though I'd visited various coasts up and down the UK and around the Mediterranean with mum, dad and James over the years, this felt different. It was like I'd seen the natural wonder of the ocean for the first time. Before, a beach had been a place to build moats, ride jet skis or burn to a crisp lathered in Hawaiian Tropic. In Florida, my eyes drank up the horizon.

I loved watching the waves shift and dance in the changing sunlight, the energy of the water out in the distance such a contrast to the gentle lapping on the beach. I wanted to bottle that feeling of serenity because I couldn't remember a time when I had ever felt so calm.

Not so soothing was the challenge of having a wee in the sea. It's not the same as when you're able-bodied and can casually stroll down to the water and pretend to have a swim.

I couldn't stroll if I tried, and certainly couldn't swim anymore. So I hatched a plan with mum. Instead of going right into the sea, we pretended we just wanted to sit on the sand and enjoy the waves splashing over our legs.

I'm sure people must have known what I was doing, but I was way past being self-conscious. My main concern was timing it right with the ebb and flow, so as not to leave mum wallowing in my effluent.

We did have a few issues when my bikini bottoms got full of sand, as emptying them involved a lot of shuffling around. I think that's when we drew most attention, but I was not going to sit there with sand in my bits. We just let the onlookers enjoy the show and had a laugh about it.

All in all, it was a great holiday. A success. We giggled through some of the difficult times and learned how we could make future trips easier.

Mum and dad didn't ask about *him* once and because he was quite far from my mind, I didn't volunteer any thoughts either. A part of me was beginning to wonder about the possibility of life without him. When I returned home in the middle of December, everything suddenly felt a bit flat.

The cracks really began to show over Christmas. He had taken some time off work, but clearly didn't want to spend it with me. Christmas Eve was a big deal in Bingley back then, everyone went out around the pubs and it was a great atmosphere. It was a bit of a tradition when people came back from university or working elsewhere that we'd all go to the White Horse or Brown Cow, then stumble across to the parish church for the midnight service.

Heaven knows what the vicar must have thought with the majority of his congregation being half-cut, but as far as I recall, nobody was ever refused entry.

It was a bit of an anti-climax for both of us to be staying in that night. He obviously had a few beers and we watched an *Only Fools and Horses* special – but not even Rodney and Del Boy could raise a smile from us.

We both knew this was not how we'd imagined our lives to be in our twenties. Miserably, we had an early night. And by that, I mean he put me to bed at about ten o'clock and stayed up drinking and watching more rubbish on TV.

Christmas Day wasn't any better. Mum and dad were away in Scotland and James was having a quiet dinner with his wife and one-year old Brennan. So us two went to The Fisherman's, a pub on Wagon Lane nearby, but sat in silence for most of our meal after falling out over something or other. We called in briefly to say 'hi' to James and his family, who were at his in-laws, then *he* took me back to the bungalow.

I could tell he was itching to go out and by then, I'd just about had enough of him.

He had a quick shower and change before heading out 'for a couple', promising not to be gone too long. Obviously, he came back drunk. The carers had clocked off because he said he'd be back for a certain time, so I couldn't even go to sleep until he returned. I physically couldn't get myself to bed.

When he eventually fell in the door, I didn't want to speak to him. He silently manhandled me into bed between hiccups then collapsed next to me and snored all night.

Being put to bed by someone drunk when you're completely sober and incapacitated is humiliating at best. It's dangerous, frankly. But by that point I was just so tired and fed up I didn't care.

The following morning, he was sheepish and hungover. It was sad to think that the year before, when I was in Chapel Allerton, I'd have given anything to have spent Christmas with him. But he'd checked out mentally from our relationship long before he plucked up the courage to end it. I didn't give him chance to do that though.

I knew he wanted out and so did I. It was just a case of getting the festive season over and done with before I could make the final break. By 1 January 2000, the deed was done.

On New Year's Eve, I went to mum and dads for a few hours while he met his friends at the pub. We agreed to both be home at eleven o'clock. At least we could be civil and see in the next millennium together. There were no carers in the house because he had again promised to be home on time, but by half past eleven there was no sign of him.

I tried ringing his mobile, but it went to voicemail. To make matters worse I needed the toilet and still couldn't manage that side of things on my own. All I could do was sit there, contemplating how on earth I was going to last before my bladder took matters into its own hands.

At a quarter to twelve I still hadn't heard from him, and despite being desperate for the loo, just wanted to be asleep.

Somehow, with all my strength, I managed to drag my chair backwards, inch by inch, using the sides of the walls in the narrow hallway to get myself into the bedroom. As I caught my breath, bladder still full and him nowhere in sight, I heard Big Ben strike midnight on the television.

Craning my neck, I caught a glimpse of the fireworks and revellers in our capital city and allowed myself a moment to cry. I was so upset to be on my own on New Year's Eve, but even more than that, I was fuming. How dare he? How absolutely bloody well DARE he?

I'd never felt fury like it. I was practically shaking with anger as I lobbed my mobile on the bed. But my rage gave me strength and I managed to get myself from my chair to the bed, in a fashion. I still don't know how.

From a face-down position, I roughly stabbed his number on speed dial and waited for it to go to voicemail, so I could tell him not to bother coming home. But he picked up. 'Where are you?' I tried to yell. 'I'm on my way home,' he slurred, and hung up.

There was absolutely no chance of me going to sleep then. My head was whirring and my bladder was bursting, but all I could do was wait.

By two o'clock he still wasn't home, so I rang him again. He said: 'I'm waiting for a taxi.' But he obviously wasn't. He didn't need a taxi because our house was within staggering distance of the pub. I said: 'Just walk home.' 'Oh, I might do,' he replied, and hung up again.

I would have given anything to be roaring drunk, walking home from a pub that night, but didn't say anything.

At three o'clock he came in, absolutely hammered. No apology. I practically had to beg him to help me go for a wee because all he wanted to do was collapse onto the bed.

Reluctantly, very sloppily, he manoeuvred me from the

Unbroken

mattress to the commode and just stared into the middle distance, swaying.

Usually at that point, he would leave the room to offer me some semblance of privacy, but this time he couldn't be bothered. 'I can't wee with you here,' I said.

'I don't care,' he replied, before flaking out on the bed.

Finally, my body took over and I managed to go, but by then he'd fallen asleep. I had to shout to wake him up and it took almost an hour to rouse him.

Eventually, he let out a huge sigh, sat up and tried to scramble me back into bed, didn't even try to get me changed into my pyjamas or offer to tuck me in. I was fully dressed, on top of the duvet at four o'clock in the morning on the very first day of the millennium.

He fell back into a drunken sleep and I waited for the carers to arrive to get me up and dressed the next morning. I'm not surprised he felt like they hated him.

When he eventually surfaced, I told him it was over. I didn't want him anywhere near me. He'd broken my body but he was not going to break my spirit.

He got down on his knees and begged me to change my mind, apologising, saying we could make it work, he was so, so sorry, he said. But that's the thing. He wasn't sorry at all. Not for that night or any other night when he'd disrespected me because he was drunk.

And he still hadn't apologised for the biggest thing of all – the crash. 'Fuck off,' I said, and meant it.

I gave him twenty-four hours alone to clear out all his belongings. He hid in the bathroom when dad picked me up, but to my parents' credit they never once said, 'I told you so'. They simply took it in their stride, offered a shoulder to cry but not dwell on and got to talking about the practicalities of my next goal.

134

When dad dropped me back the next day, the house felt empty but a lot better. I noticed *he* had even taken my engagement ring, which I'd paid for. But instead of feeling cross and sad about that, I felt oddly free. I shook my head in disbelief about what I'd been through since August 1998.

By casting him out of my life, I began to realise that I was totally in control of what happened to me next.

I could choose.

All I had to do was get as well as I could, use what strength I had to the best of my ability and take it one step at a time.

In many ways, getting rid of *him* was the true beginning of my healing process. But it wasn't until 2020, after the first meeting with my therapist, that I started truly questioning why I had ever convinced myself that such a relationship was healthy in the first place.

17

•

A Different Direction

NOT LONG AFTER breaking free, the wheels were set in motion for my final compensation agreement. It's strange to think that if *he* and I had stayed together, he might have actually benefitted from my pay-out.

For a crime *he* committed.

Dad did all the legwork, but there was a lot of involvement from insurers, lawyers, solicitors and barristers. I've never spoken outside my family about the actual amount of remuneration, but we do feel the outcome was fair.

Obviously, nobody would choose to go through what I did, but I have to say that even though my life was turned absolutely on its head for a good while, I've had a much more varied and adventurous one than I think would have done if I hadn't been in the car crash.

I escaped an inevitable divorce for starters. I am still child-free (never wanted children, but would've felt pressure from him) and, in all likelihood, would not have learned to pole dance or have had chance to walk on fire.

'Compensation' gets a bad press. When people hear the word it conjures up images of layabouts trying to claim for fake whiplash injuries, or accidents at work where they have allegedly fallen off a ladder. But for we who couldn't live our lives without it – it is essential.

My compensation has brought stability and peace of mind. It has allowed me to have a roof over my head, money to feed and clothe myself and, almost as importantly, given me time and choices.

Like most people who work for a living, I get to decide if I save for a holiday, or splurge and buy a new handbag.

It has enabled me to enable myself – paid for one-to-one personal training to strengthen my body. It has facilitated trips abroad to feel sunshine on my mending bones.

It has bought me a car, which means I am independent, and more recently it has meant I can engage in some long-overdue therapy to hopefully, finally, lay some demons to rest from my teenage years.

The whole process of compensation is long and drawn out. The one thing we did have on our side though was that he admitted liability form the start, so there was no battle to be fought there.

One particularly difficult stumbling block was the fact that the rehabilitation unit in Chapel Allerton claimed to have lost all my X-rays. And if there is one thing insurers want, it's undeniable evidence.

Initially, mum and dad tried to deal with that on their own – there were about forty of the things altogether. After weeks of waiting, mum lost patience and marched up to the main desk and demanded to see the person who had been in charge of my care, along with the head of the X-ray team.

'Where the bloody hell are they?' she screamed. 'Surely to God, something else must have been X-rayed while Georgina's been in your care – so haven't you even got some more recent ones? What are you hiding?'

There was a lot of shuffling and looking at the floor. Excuses ranged from them being unavailable due to them being used by student doctors for research, to them being in the process of being put on to microfiche, which apparently was done by a company off site.

Mum said: 'Right, let's get the microfiche then. How do we go about doing that?' There were so many ifs and buts that she had to walk away before she lost it.

Dad began proceedings by contacting a law firm in Leeds who had a litigation office. He'd had dealings with them before in a work capacity so was hopeful that, with some proper legal clout, Chapel Allerton might find my X-rays again and they could start moving the process along.

He set up a meeting with the solicitor, himself, mum and the head honcho at Chapel Allerton. Dad wanted the team there to know the Hurst family were not a pushover and that we would fight them to the nth degree to get what we needed. But when it came to it, when they were all finally sat around the table, dad's solicitor appeared to be more on Chapel Allerton's side than ours. Dad said it was like he was a poacher turned gamekeeper, not fighting for us in any way.

It was so frustrating for my parents because they were still trying to come to terms with the accident and the state it had left me in.

It wasn't just a business transaction, a lawsuit involving non-payment of fees for example, they were fighting for me and what I deserved. They were dealing with a very emotional case because it involved their daughter, and how I was going to be able to manage for the rest of my life.

At this point, I was still reliant on care assistance around the clock. It must have been exhausting for them having to invest all that time energy into the case, simply to ensure I'd be safe and secure both physically and financially.

Dad couldn't look at this solicitor. He was fuming and made no attempt to hide his feelings. As soon as the meeting came to a close, he went straight to the solicitor's head office and verbally gave them both barrels.

Within twenty-four hours, the guy had been removed from our case and we were appointed a new solicitor called Steve. He was absolutely brilliant and worked tirelessly on my behalf until the case was finalised.

The first thing Steve did was come to visit me. Right from the start he had that personal touch and could see for himself just what I'd been through. He asked me lots of questions, properly listened to the answers, and I was included in the entire process from then on. We all felt reassured that he was invested in us and our case.

After initial talks, Steve said that to stand a real chance of getting what we deserved, we would need a barrister. But that in itself can be a lengthy procedure too.

I didn't realise, but you have to apply for a barrister – and pay them around a thousand pounds just for them to consider taking on your case. But Steve got everything sorted and sent our case notes off, along with a cheque, and we were appointed someone who really wanted to fight *his* insurance company, irrespective of the fact that we had no X-rays.

These barristers really know their stuff. They're able to break everything down into specific injuries or increments and then gather it all together.

They have lists of what amounts you should be awarded for certain injuries, ranging from twisted ankles to broken necks. Then they take into consideration the whole impact of those injuries together and how they will encumber the rest of your life.

They look at all the income you may have earned over your lifetime, and any promotions you will miss and pensions you won't be able to contribute into to.

They assess all your medical costs, from operations to round-the-clock care, for the rest of your life. And they take your mental health into account too, the knock-on effect all this could have on a person's happiness. There are so many different elements to iron out.

The barrister negotiates everything at the end and it's all done on neutral territory, in a couple of hotel meeting rooms, somewhere between the barrister and the insurance company's location.

I'll never forget the day it was all finalised. There was mum, dad, myself, Steve and our barrister in one room, and the insurance company and their barrister in another.

There was a lot of to-ing and fro-ing as the negotiations began. Mum, dad, Steve and I sat in this bland, uninspiring place, trying to take our minds off what was happening and not get too impatient. They all chatted amongst themselves about the weather, what holiday plans they had, basically anything apart from the job in hand.

All I could focus on was the dust on the vertical blinds at the window. I kept wondering how many other people like me had sat in this room, gazing out at the car park below while two men in suits battled out their fate.

We were interrupted by the door opening. Our barrister said the insurance company had refused our suggestion, but had a counter-offer for us to consider. We did that for a nano-second, then told them to come up with something better.

When our barrister left the room this time, the silence wasn't filled with small talk. We knew what we'd come for and we weren't leaving until it had been agreed. It felt tense, I noticed Steve getting a bit jittery, but that could have been the extra two cups of coffee he'd consumed in the process.

Through the blinds I could see the heavy grey sky as spatters of sleet began to hit the window. The heating had been ramped up as snow was forecast and I noticed mum put her hand on the radiator and then quickly draw it back.

The tension and temperature combined to make for a very stuffy atmosphere. We were all beginning to feel like we had cabin fever. Every time we heard footsteps approaching the thick wooden door, we all sat a bit straighter, expecting our barrister to enter.

Over the hour, I counted twelve incidences of people walking up to, and then straight past, our entrance. Our room was near the lift. I tried to pass time by imagining what the people looked like by the sound of their shoes on the corridor. Fast, heavy strides equalled busy businessman. Stop-start shuffling accompanied by a wheeling noise meant an elderly couple making the most of a midweek deal. The cleaner was an easy one – rustling bin bags and UHT milk refills.

Finally, the door opened and our barrister smiled. 'I think you'll like this offer,' he said. He sat down and laid out the details, talking us through it.

We were all hot and hungry, but hung on every word. When he finished, mum, dad, Steve and myself all looked at each other. The barrister was right. We were happy with what he'd negotiated on our behalf and agreed to sign.

After all the necessary paperwork was completed, we were free to leave. The barrister was the first to exit, saying he wanted to be on the next train to London. He shook our hands, told us a date for the final settlement and left. Then Steve shook all our hands and made his way to the lift.

Mum, dad and myself just looked at each other and dad

said: 'Right, well that's that then.' I don't know what we were expecting, for some kind of alarm to sound and a load of ticker tape to start falling from the ceiling? A sense of closure maybe? In all reality, it was a bit of an anti-climax. It hadn't sunk in. We were all a bit numb.

We left the room, mum pressed the button for the lift and dad wheeled me in. When the doors closed, mum hit 'R' for reception and we descended in silence.

When they opened, it was with a distinct drop in temperature. The cool air was welcome on my face. I took a deep breath and, as I exhaled, felt my body relax.

I'd obviously been a lot more tense than I thought. Mum caught my eye and smiled. We knew that from then on, I could make my own choices without fear of wondering whether or not I could afford it. It truly was a weight off my shoulders that I hadn't even realised I'd been carrying.

We decided to go to the nearest place we could find for food and ended up at one of these chain burger joints, which you usually find near motorway hotels. In hindsight, we ought to have splashed out on somewhere swankier and ordered champagne, but we just needed sustenance.

It was only after we'd all demolished our burgers that we sat back and properly looked at each other.

Dad had tears in his eyes. I think he was just relieved that his daughter could now have a life that wasn't just safe and secure – but happy and possibly adventurous.

He'd done his bit and done us all proud.

Mum drained the last of her white wine and went outside for a cigarette. I asked for the bill.

This one was most definitely on me.

18

•

World of Water

HE MOVED ON swiftly with his life. I heard on the grapevine that it wasn't long before he was out on the pull in Bingley again. Good riddance.

With him out of the picture, I was able to focus my strength on improving my body and after a lot of research, I found an amazing private residential rehabilitation centre called Abbey Gisburn, on the Lancashire border. It ticked every box.

It's still there and quite fancy – set in two hundred acres of parkland. Metaphorically a million miles away from Chapel Shithole.

When we drove up to the entrance, everything looked inviting. It had a stately air, was welcoming, light and clean. It resembled a hotel, the sort that would have a golf club attached. I knew immediately that I was going to be a lot happier there and make plenty of progress.

Unbroken

Even my bedroom was lovely. Pretty curtains instead of functional blinds, duvet covers that didn't feel jaded and carpet underfoot that wasn't too thick for a wheelchair, but still gave it a homely touch.

I had my own bathroom, which made a huge difference. It was spacious and functional with the right fixtures to make it easier for me to get in and out of a bath or shower, but it was also decorated nicely in modern colours, so I didn't feel like I was in an institution.

The staff were friendly and approachable, keen to help and I didn't get a sense that they were clockwatching.

The facilities were second to none and kitted out with everything you could imagine to enable me to become more 'me' again. I embraced it all. There was hydrotherapy, speech therapy, therapy-therapy, equipment with hoists, weights, parallel bars, ropes, pulleys, the lot.

If there was any remote chance of any part of a body being healed in that place, they had the knowledge, patience and wherewithal to make it happen.

My favourite treatment was the one in the water – hydrotherapy. I used to love swimming as a child and have many happy memories of holidays splashing in pools with family and friends. In fact, I learned to swim on holiday, in a place called Cortijo Grande in Spain. We've still got an old cine-camera film of me doing it.

Mum and dad had hired a villa with two other families; there was Glynis and Stephen with their son Robert, plus Martin and Francis and their daughters, Alison and Julia.

On Wednesday 29 July 1981, the day of Charles and Diana's royal wedding at St Paul's Cathedral, the adults dragged the television outside under the canopy and had it on first thing in the morning for the build-up.

Robert was my age and could already swim, so I was

144

absolutely determined that I was going to master it as soon as I could. Mum encouraged me do a width in the shallow end with arm bands on, then each time she'd let a little bit more air out of them and I'd go a bit deeper until, finally, I managed to do it on my own.

I was absolutely chuffed to bits – especially since my brother still couldn't swim at that stage. Nothing like a bit of sibling oneupmanship.

Nowadays, every time there is something in the media about Charles and Di's wedding, I am immediately reminded of that time abroad, my first width without assistance – and the look of envy on James's face.

At Abbey Gisburn, I tried to learn to swim again from scratch. My mind could remember exactly what to do, but my body was physically unable to follow the signals.

It had come so naturally before, but now felt like a completely different challenge. My physiotherapist was amazing. I can't for the life of me remember his name, but he was Australian, mid-twenties, with short dark hair and often wore a white polo shirt with navy trousers.

He was match-fit and very easy on the eye. In another life, or situation, I certainly wouldn't have kicked him out of bed for farting. He was adamant that I took one step at a time and told me not to beat myself up for being unable to keep afloat without assistance.

He pressed home the importance of simply just being in the water and feeling the resistance of it against my limbs to begin with. I thought, at least I'm using a woggle rather than armbands – that would have been humiliating.

Getting my cozzie on was a right palaver, another task I couldn't do on my own. It involved someone else helping me out of my clothes and into the bathing suit.

I also had to make sure I'd had a wee before the whole

rigmarole began because getting in and out of the pool was quite a task too. I could hardly do a Clearwater beach scenario and pee in the shallow end if nature unexpectedly called, could I?

I had to be hoisted into the water too, which was a three-person job, if you included me. One to get me into the hoist and lower me down – plus another one ready to get me in the water. But once in, I loved the feeling of weightlessness.

It was always so warm, like bath temperature, and it really did feel relaxing. The jet streams helped keep me afloat as the physiotherapist manoeuvred me around the pool.

With guidance, I was able to stretch and bend muscles in the water that I wouldn't have been able to do on dry land.

It was also good cardiovascular exercise, because although I felt all floaty McFloatface, I did have to apply myself physically. It must have worked because I was always starving after a session in the hydrotherapy pool.

No matter how long I spent in the water, it always seemed to take twice as long to get out and dressed.

I'm so relieved I can take care of all those aspects for myself now, but at the time, towelling my bits was nigh on impossible because I couldn't reach around my back to properly grip the towel for long enough. But those sessions set me off on the right path and, when I left Abbey Gisburn, I found a swimming instructor called Gemma at my local fitness centre who continued to help me.

Gemma was fantastic. We're still friends now. She's just one of these smiley people who brings out the best in you.

Her hair was in a cute little dark cropped style at the time, for practicality as much as fashion, but it really suited her. And she was taller than me at five foot six, which helped a lot when we were in the water.

She boosted my confidence no end and soon got me

doing widths using one of the woggles. Gemma was always beside me in the water in case I lost my purchase, but after a lot of work, I could keep my head above the surface without her assistance.

My arms were getting stronger, but there was no way I could have treaded water because one leg was stronger than the other and I'd have ended up going round in circles, spiralling to the bottom of the pool.

Unfortunately, my swimming confidence only lasted a few years. Now I'm petrified of not just open water but pools as well, following an incident in Scotland in 2004.

I was in a swanky spa hotel with mum and dad over Christmas and New Year. It happened on the same day as the Indian Ocean tsunami, Boxing Day.

On Christmas Day, the hotel restaurant had really gone to town with dinner, ensuring the atmosphere was just the right mixture of classy but jovial for our four courses. The tables were set beautifully, the tree looked amazing and carols played in the background. It really was a treat.

As a result, we could hardly move afterwards because we hadn't said 'no' to one single thing, even down to the cake, cheese and after dinner choccies. The next morning, we decided we'd make an effort to shift some festive lard down by the pool.

Although I enjoyed being in the water, I was nowhere near being able to swim again without a woggle, and still relied on having another person next to me in the pool for support.

Mum and I went in together and dad took a seat by the side. There weren't any woggles, but we got around it by mum using her arms to support me under my stomach.

We tried one width and it seemed to work. When we reached the edge, we both caught our breath and decided to go for a second one, but nearer the deep end. It was a slow process and very tiring for the pair of us.

I was about two metres away from the side of the pool and mum thought I looked pretty done in, so she tried to move her body away to make it easier to pull me to the edge.

But I didn't realise she was helping. I thought she was leaving me and began to panic, which in turn meant I lost any balance I had. I began to feel myself sinking.

It was so frightening, gulping in water as I worked my arms to try to bring my head to the surface, brutally aware that my legs couldn't do what I wanted them to do.

I could feel myself getting lower, my eyes wide open in the water as everything around me blurred. It can't have gone on for long, but the fear will last for ever.

With it being a private pool, there was no lifeguard, but as soon as mum realised what was happening, she was underneath me, bouncing on the bottom of the pool floor, trying to keep me afloat. It will have taken all her strength to keep me on top of her.

To add insult to injury, her hair got a soaking, which she hates.

While we were having what must have looked like a tussle with the Loch Ness Monster, dad was shouting for help. He's not a good swimmer himself, so couldn't jump in and save us. But people nearby thought he was messing around and they were laughing.

I honestly thought I was going to die – again, and by the time the alarm had been raised and other spa users realised it was serious, mum had somehow managed to get me to the water's edge.

Dad grabbed my hands and held on until he and mum could lift me out. I was coughing and spluttering, trying to catch my breath again and mum looked utterly shell-shocked.

Dad ended up sopping wet as well, as he knelt down and held me until my breathing steadied.

That was a Boxing Day I won't forget in a hurry.

Later that evening, in my hotel room, I switched on the TV to catch the news and saw those horrific scenes from the west coast of northern Sumatra, epicentre of the disaster, and beyond. Indonesia, Sri Lanka, India, Maldives and Thailand sustained the worst damage, all of it caused by an undersea earthquake with a magnitude of 9.1. It is now estimated that a quarter of a million people died across a dozen countries.

As I watched the footage of those people clinging to debris, trying to climb higher on to roof tops and seeing the sea decimate villages I couldn't imagine the terror they must have felt. Families separated, young children and parents unable to reach each other's hands and that certain panic of not knowing if those pulled under would ever resurface.

I'm not in any way religious, but that night I said a silent prayer for all those people. My dreams were plagued with floods and a sense of drowning for weeks afterwards.

I haven't been to a swimming pool since 2004 and even now feel terrified of falling into water. Mum would really like me to get over my fear and have some more lessons, but it's one thing I've dug my heels in about. I just can't.

At Abbey Gisburn, exercise was varied, with the hydrotherapy pool only taking up about twenty per cent of my fitness regime.

A number of physiotherapists put me through my paces in the gym and showed no mercy – for my own sake. Even though it was tough, it wasn't painful but it was mentally exhausting.

Most people don't even think about walking, it's just second nature. But after an accident like mine there are two issues.

One, you aren't just re-learning to walk, like you'd forgotten and needed a refresher course, you're having to utilise different muscles in your body because the ones which used to do the job are banjaxed.

And two, you are having to build up that strength from nothing, which means re-training your brain to get it used to firing new signals to different muscles. On top of that, you need the willpower to chuffing well do it.

Like anyone, some days I just wasn't in the mood. However, giving up was never an option I entertained.

There were people of varying ages and abilities in the gym at Abbey Gisburn. Some were way ahead of me, which gave me a goal to aim for.

Others were a lot, lot worse and I wondered if they'd ever make it out of the room, never mind out of the building.

I've no idea what they thought of me, where they'd have placed me on the 'likelihood to put one foot in front of the other again' scale, but at the time, I didn't care. All I wanted to do was walk.

It took absolutely everything I had in me eventually to manage a couple of steps using the parallel bars.

I spent months of work on my upper body in the gym to enable me to hold myself upright. It was punishing, but every night I went to sleep happy in the knowledge that I was improving, heading in the right direction of recovery.

My dexterity was getting better too, so mealtimes were slowly changing from an event I had to endure to a part of the day I could look forward to.

Cutting up food was still difficult, but I could now coax a knife and fork into the right areas and bring food up to my own mouth. All these were small steps but, collectively, they combined to start making me feel whole again.

I can't fully explain the emotions I went through when

I eventually managed those two steps with the bars. It wasn't fast, more a slow drag as I heaved one foot in front of the other. They felt so heavy. Imagine having a small boulder balanced on top of each foot, with your legs being as thin as twigs, and then someone telling you to walk straight through a waist-high snow drift.

That's what it was like, trying day after day and then, one morning, I just did it. My Australian physiotherapist was in front, near enough to catch me if I needed catching, and we were face-to-face.

My muscles had bulked enough in both my upper and lower body, so all I had to do was apply my mind and try to co-ordinate everything to work together.

Slowly, my right foot edged forward, still dragging a little on the floor, but it was going in the right direction. We smiled at each other. I'd done it. I was shattered.

There was no getting off lightly at Abbey Gisburn. 'Now the left foot,' he coaxed. 'Come on George, you can do it. Focus. Think. You know what you've got to do.'

With absolutely all my strength and determination I looked him in the eye and slowly heaved the left side of my body forward, enabling me to use the momentum to take another step.

For a split second my left foot left the floor, moved forward, landing in front of my right one. It felt like a miracle, it really did.

Both of us had tears in our eyes as he caught me in a hug and said: 'You've done it George. You've bloody gone and done it.'

Those two steps gave me such hope. If I could do that, I thought, there was nothing stopping me from slowly building up to taking more steps, then learning to use crutches and then, finally, becoming independent again.

So much for slowly.

Once I'd got a taste for movement, I couldn't wait to do more. Just a few months afterwards, mum was on one of her regular visits.

As she pulled up in the car park, I appeared from around the corner of the building, on crutches. I'd made it all the way around the outside and mum was absolutely thrilled.

She hadn't been expecting it, so it was such a perfect surprise for her – and the catalyst for me to think about moving out of rehab and into my own home again.

19

•

Gritting My Teeth

AFTER GOD KNOWS how many viewings and discussions about accessibility, I had an offer accepted on a suitable bungalow in Bingley.

The location near friends and family was perfect, and once we'd let our interiors doyen (Lou, from ICU) loose on it, I couldn't wait to move in.

By early 2001, everything was in place, including a care package to ensure I had help at hand around the clock.

The staff at Abbey Gisburn had done so much to get me to this point that I felt a bit overwhelmed when they all waved me and mum off; but as soon as mum pulled out of the driveway, she turned and said, 'Don't look back, George. It's time for pastures new.' Typical.

It took me seven whole years from the day of the crash to gain enough strength and coordination to be able to walk a mile, with crutches. But as soon as I'd put my left foot in front of my right at Abbey Gisburn, I knew I had to set myself a goal to smash.

At the time, it sounded like madness. I could still barely hold myself upright but having that target pushed me through. In the back of my mind, I still heard the voice of Dr Doom telling me I'd never walk again and I wanted to prove him wrong if it was the last thing I ever did.

I also realised I'd focus better if I told everyone about my plan – I couldn't back out then because I'd look a right numpty. I decided to do it for charity, get sponsorship and enlist the help of the local newspaper, the *Telegraph & Argus*.

The editor liked my story and I made the front page on Monday 9 August 2004. Half of it was taken up with a photograph of me in my chair, while the other half said in huge capital letters: 'I WILL WALK ONCE MORE'.

Under the subheading 'Paralysed paramedic vows to complete charity event', my story read:

A woman paramedic who was paralysed in a road accident today set herself the remarkable challenge of walking a mile for charity.

George Hurst, 32, suffered horrific injuries when the car she was in crashed on a moorland road near Keighley six years ago. It took firefighters an hour to cut her free from the wreckage in which she broke her neck and her leg, crushed her pelvis and suffered massive internal injuries including brain-stem damage which left her confined to a wheelchair for the rest of her life.

Injury experts said she would never walk again but using special crutches she is determined to complete the challenge next year.

George, of Eldwick, has slowly and painfully

started to piece together her life since the accident – although she knows she will never have back the paramedic job she loved.

She has had to teach herself to speak and write again and needs the support of full-time carers to carry out day-to-day tasks. But she is still determined to help others and will next month start a part-time course at Craven College, Skipton, in a quest to become a trauma counsellor to help other accident victims.

'I know I'll never be a paramedic again but I loved my job. It was perfect for me but now it's impossible so I've had to find another way of helping people heal as best as I can and that will be through counselling.'

George says she owes a lot to the staff at the health club where she trains almost every day. Health club general manager, Ceri Morgan said: 'She's an exceptionally brave person. The dedication she shows here will help her achieve her goals.'

Her brother James said: 'She is a people's person and always has been. The accident hasn't changed that. Not everyone could have pulled through like she has and still manage to stay so optimistic. She is an inspiration.'

Georgina Simmons, who is a senior nurse at the unit in unit at St James's Hospital, Leeds, said: 'We feel heartened that there is a really positive side to critical care and are pleased George is doing so well. She's a great role model to others.'

George also paid tribute to her family, especially her mum, Heather, who have stood by her.

'I'm proof that there is light at the end of the tunnel,' she said.

So that kind of sealed the deal really. I was front page news and there was no backing out now.

I was going to do the walk around a place called Yeadon Tarn. I chose that location because it is flat, circular and quite a pretty walk around the perimeter.

There is a children's play area, which usually has an ice cream van nearby, and plenty of places to park. It's as popular with families and dog-walkers as it is with aeroplane enthusiasts, who enjoy a perfect viewing position of the Leeds-Bradford Airport runway.

It was just over a year after that front-page story that I actually did it, on Saturday 10 September 2005. To get there, I had trained like mad.

As well as going to the gym, I went to Yeadon Tarn with various carers to build my route slowly. We split it into sections for me to master before putting it all together. I began by doing about an eighth, then a quarter and so on until after threequarters I knew that I was as ready as I would ever be to go the full mile. I didn't want to do the very last bit until the main event, because I thought it would give me that extra push to aim for.

My carers were really supportive and patient during all the practice, but it was good in the sense that we had a plan and a timetable to work to, which helped the weeks fly by.

When it came to the day of the mile, we were really lucky with the weather, considering it was early September.

There is never any guarantee of mercury rising above zero in West Yorkshire, but the sun was actually shining and the ground was dry, hugely important when you are relying on crutches. I didn't want a ground full of slippery, soggy leaves and big puddles to negotiate. I could have ended up doing a *Bambi-on-Ice*. But just as importantly it wasn't windy, as a big gust has the potential to topple me over.

So many of my friends and family came out in support. They walked alongside and stopped when I needed to have a rest or take a drink.

Simple words of encouragement like: 'We know you can do it George.' 'Dig deep.' 'One foot in front of the other' and, crucially, 'Think of the ice cream at the end,' did so much to buoy me up when I felt I was flagging. I felt like Forrest Gump in slow motion.

It honestly was so unbelievably tiring, the hardest physical trial I'd ever faced. Nothing like the aerobics classes I'd been to when younger, or cross-country races I'd smashed running for the school team.

This challenge was in a league of its own. Every part of my body hurt, including my brain. My hands were blistered because of the weight being pushed onto them as I gripped the handles of my crutches. My wrists were throbbing, my ankles ached, and it felt like I had a sack of rubble dragging down my sweaty back.

I knew nobody would have minded too much if I just stopped and said I couldn't quite make it to the finish line, that they were with me no matter how far I managed to walk, yet I felt I not only owed it to myself but also to the charities due to benefit if I finished the task. I just had to get my head down, grit my teeth and get on with it.

When it came to the very final section, about an eighth of a mile, I got a second wind from somewhere.

Perhaps it was the adrenalin or the fact that other visitors to the tarn realised what was happening and began to cheer me on too.

I could see a mum pushing two toddlers on the swings, encouraging them to clap and wave at me as they swished up and down.

We made our way past an old couple taking a rest on a

bench, who picked up their walking sticks and joined the back of our group.

A man walking an assortment of dogs slowed his pace and tagged along too. It was quite surreal and an incredible boost.

Then, at the very last push, I lifted my head and saw dad standing behind the finishing line with my brother James and my seven-year old nephew.

Brennan's full attention was on the '99' ice cream cone his grandad had just bought him. As he devoured it one big mouthful at a time, dad just stared at me, with his right arm outstretched, holding another 99 just out of my reach.

'You'd better get this before it melts,' he smiled. James put his arm around Brennan and urged: 'Come ON, George, nearly there.'

I felt so happy taking those last few steps. I couldn't believe they'd thought to go ahead to coax me over the line with a vanilla cone.

I didn't know whether to laugh or cry when my right foot, then my left finally made it to the end.

Everyone gathered around me and they were cheering, shouting 'Well done, George. You've done it, you've done it.'

Slumping onto a bench I threw my sticks to the ground and reached out for my ice cream from dad.

The coolness on my tongue and sweet sugary taste combined to create quite a kick. I threw my head back. It was heaven. Mum plonked down next to me and grinned.

'Well done, George – what's next?'

I had completed it in fifty-seven minutes and twenty-five seconds, raising five thousand pounds for St James's Hospital and a charity called The Smart Risk Foundation, whose aim is to reduce preventable injuries through education in schools.

I got such a buzz out of that achievement and knew I wasn't going to stop there. I wanted to do so much more to help others and myself in the process, so began researching charities that combined fundraising with a physical challenge – and I found loads.

It also set me on the path to doing more for The smart Risk Foundation, where I learned to try and overcome the embarrassment of my voice by speaking about my experiences to hundreds of schoolchildren.

20
•
Confidence Boost

KNOWING HOW BRUTAL schoolkids can be, I wanted to give myself as much of a fighting chance as possible for my first engagement.

If I was going into a stuffy assembly hall to tell my cautionary tale of boy-racing, I wanted to feel confident inside and out. My crutches and speech were already big enough targets for abuse, so I didn't want them to think I was a scaredy-cat on top of that.

Somehow, kids can always sense a teacher's nerves and it only takes one pupil to bring it to the attention of the rest of the class. Once that happens, it's curtains.

One person who always makes me feel confident is my beautician, Suzanne, who I've been going to since I was about sixteen. Before my first school talk, I booked myself in for the full works at her salon, Mirror Mirror, in Bingley.

Suzanne understands how important it is for me to

look as good as I can, because if I look good, I feel good. In fact, as soon as I possibly could after the accident, I got back into the habit of having beauty treatments.

Just because I could hardly move didn't mean I was going to give in to bushy eyebrows or rug-like nether regions. I still wanted things to be trim. But it wasn't easy logistically, so when I first came out of hospital and was living with mum and dad, Suzanne offered to come to our house instead.

We used a sun lounger in the kitchen as a salon bed and often ended up having a right good giggle. We usually had a coffee first, while the wax warmed up and talked about everything and anything.

She used to worry she might hurt me whilst angling me into tricky positions for those hard-to-reach areas, but she was always gentle. I'd be saying: 'Don't worry. Get that leg bent backwards, shift that buttock up a bit...'

Suzanne had been good friends with mum and dad for years, so she came with them to visit me in hospital at Jimmy's a few times. Not to do any treatments at that stage, obviously, but just to say hello. I think she had a real shock. She still gets quite emotional when we talk about it now. She says it wasn't just the tubes and the halo on my head, but the fact that I could only really signal yes or no by sticking my tongue out.

The bizarre thing is, Suzanne had heard about the car crash on the day it happened, but didn't realise it involved me. Her parents-in-law, Margaret and Gordon, were very good friends with the lady who *he* ploughed into.

Suzanne received a phone call from Margaret days before she found out I was the one who'd been crushed up and put on a life support machine. She couldn't believe it.

By the time I was fit and able enough to speak in schools, I could get myself to the salon independently again.

Unbroken

Well, I could get myself outside the salon, but getting inside involved a bit of creative thought. Mirror Mirror was situated at the top of a long narrow flight of stairs and there wasn't a lift. Suzanne had a brainwave. She was friendly with a guy called Paul who owned the carpet shop below and managed to negotiate a space in his storeroom at the back of his shop on the ground floor.

Can you imagine what we must have looked like?

There I was, wedged between lino samples and rolls of Axminister while Suzanne warmed the wax pot in their kitchen. There was no special light for spotting those tricky hairs, so it was a case of putting all the strip lights on and turning the head torch up to full beam. It was a scream.

When I smell new carpet now, I always think back to those days. I will never look at a tufted rug the same again.

One day, I turned up in a big woolly hat in the middle of summer. I was wearing it because I was trying to cover what looked like an enormous second head growing behind my ear. It was the surgical balloon which had been inserted to stretch my skin, to help repair my bald patch. But Suzanne just carried on as normal.

When I told her why I was wearing the hat, she didn't respond like most people would by tilting her head to one side and looking at me sympathetically. She just simply said: 'Why should I feel sorry for you, when you don't feel sorry for yourself?' It was exactly the right thing to say.

She is completely on my side, one of my best champions. If I'm ever in the reception area at Mirror Mirror now and she sees someone slyly looking at my sticks, she deliberately starts asking how my pole dancing is going.

Or if they strike up a conversation with me, but in a slow voice, Suzanne trots over and asks me something normally, so they realise.

She reckons I should be on television and radio, sharing my story and inspiring others, and is convinced I will end up on a billboard in America in a pole dancing pose.

Like all my other friends, she also thinks I deserve to meet an amazing man who will join me on all my adventures.

One step at a time.

After a confidence boosting visit to Mirror Mirror and a final check through of my notes, I was all set for my first school talk. They were teenagers, so I'd tried to make sure the pitch was just right, friendly but not cringey, as if I wanted to be down with them.

I needed to get a serious message across without preaching. I'd had a few practices at home, but if I knew one thing about school assemblies it was if you hadn't piqued their interest in the first ten seconds, you might as well hobble off through a pile of tumbleweed. Teenagers are undoubtedly one of the toughest crowds.

It was October 2005, just a month after walking a mile and only a year since I'd learned to drive an automatic car again. The school was in Cumbria, so the journey took me the best part of a couple of hours along the A65 and M6.

My time slot was just after lunch, but I'd given myself plenty of breathing space. I'm a stickler for punctuality.

I was tuned to Radio One , enjoying listening to Kaiser Chiefs' 'I Predict a Riot' and Kanye West's 'Gold Digger'. As my hands tapped along on the steering wheel, the thought struck me – how far I had come since 1998.

Nobody must have thought back then that I would drive again. They didn't even know if I'd breathe unaided.

Pulling into the school car park, I searched for a spot for a while before remembering that I was disabled and therefore qualified for the best parking space. Take your perks where you can get them, I say.

Unbroken

Playground noises drifted over the low wall as I switched my engine off and grabbed my crutches. A handful of geeky boys gathered in a corner, looking awkward, while teenage girls, linking arms, wandered the perimeter of the yard, flicking their hair and scoping out the talent on the football pitch. Two bored teachers were chatting to each other, mugs of coffee in hand, with half an eye out for any dramas.

I wondered if any of those young girls had been through what I had at their age. Were they hiding a dark secret too? Putting on a brave face for fear of re-opening a wound which might never heal again?

They looked happy enough, but then so had I, before everything threatened to come tumbling out in a biology class. I took a moment to gather my thoughts, breathed in, and rammed that flashback right into the recess of my mind, where it belonged.

I made my way on crutches to reception where I was asked to take a seat and wait for the year leader, who would be with me shortly.

I'm sure all schools smell the same at lunchtime; mince and onions, sugary custard and always an underlying note of sweaty trainers. When the bell went for the end of break, teachers emerged from the staff room looking like they were bracing themselves for a long afternoon of learning. Lanyards swung and exercise books were piled high in one hand, as the last dregs of coffee were slurped from a cherished mug with the other.

I heard the faint echo of a telling-off in the distance for an untucked-in shirt. I was undoubtably back in school, only now I was older and a little bit wiser.

Teachers have that way of being able to shift between personas, almost without pausing, depending on who they are addressing. Mrs Armstrong, the year leader, segued from stern and all-knowing after the shirt incident to smiley and gentle when she saw me. 'Georgina?' she enquired. I nodded. 'It's so lovely to meet you. You're such and inspiration and I'm sure my year group will really gain a lot. I'll show you the hall and let you get settled. We're due to start in about ten minutes and the students will begin filing in, in about five. Is there anything you need? A cup of tea? Glass of water?'

I sensed she was a little nervous for me. Perhaps the teenagers really were going to be a nightmare. But then I reminded myself that they were getting out of normal lessons for this, so should be at least a little bit lenient on me.

'Just a glass of water would be great, please,' I replied, and began making my way to the front corner of the hall.

A-level artwork adorned the walls, self-portraits in the style of Andy Warhol, close-ups of ashtrays with burning cigarettes, a papier-mâché horse's head mounted on a plinth.

I was rubbish at art at school, but hadn't minded the classes because at least I got to talk to my friends. I never really progressed much further than stick men. When we were asked to draw the view from our bedroom window, I literally just did a sketch of my curtains.

But some of these looked quite good.

I plonked down on the chair, leant my crutches against the low table next to me and waited. Mrs Armstrong re-joined me with the water and took her place behind the lectern.

The hall began to fill up with teenagers and as they entered, I could see them looking over at me, trying to size me up, wondering what I might say. Other than my crutches, there was no way of knowing I was disabled, but they'd obviously been briefed.

'Right everybody, settle down,' Mrs Armstrong began. 'As you know, Georgina has kindly come in today to share her inspirational story of recovery following a wholly avoidable car accident. I don't want any noise at all during her talk and want you to listen very carefully. Georgina is happy to answer any questions you might have afterwards, but put your hand up and don't shout out. Right Georgina, are you ready?' I nodded.

I grabbed my sticks and slowly got to my feet. I wanted them to see the physical impact of what *he* had done before I began to speak.

I took about ten steps to the middle of the stage, where the school had placed another chair if I needed it. I didn't say anything as I walked, just let the noise of the rubber stoppers on the bottom of my crutches do the talking for me.

When I reached centre stage I looked up to a sea of expectant faces. You could hear a pin drop.

'My fiancé thought it would be a good idea to race his friends on a main road, while I was a passenger in his car,' I began. 'It was the worst idea he ever had. It's taken me seven years to learn to walk again and as you can tell, I'm now left sounding like a bit of a tit.'

They laughed at that. I wasn't sure I could use the word 'tit', but it broke the ice. I went on to tell them about all my injuries, the fact I had to be resuscitated four times in all and had kissed goodbye to a career I absolutely loved.

There were photographs to hand around, showing the state of the car and my injuries not long after the crash.

The girls reacted differently to the boys. They tended to be more sympathetic, putting themselves in my shoes and imagining what it must be like not to be able to run around or do the same things as your friends.

The boys sat up straighter when they heard the word prison. Boys at that age think they're invincible. They're hardwired to take risks when testosterone kicks in and can't see danger or consequences. It's all about impressing their peers at any cost. I could see the cogs turning in their heads. It's one thing to be told to drive safely or not get in a car with a potential lunatic, but quite another to see the repercussions first-hand.

I was the indisputable evidence of a bad decision. I think they were quite taken aback, but not as much as I was when they not only engaged by asking lots of questions, but also gave me a huge round of applause when I'd finished.

A few of them even approached me separately on the way out and told me I was amazing.

Mrs Armstrong was thrilled. As the pupils filed back out after the bell, she turned to me and thanked me profusely. 'You've done something really special today, Georgina,' she said. 'This year group has been a particularly challenging one for us, but you held their attention throughout and gave them a lot to think about. I honestly think the penny dropped with some of those boys and hope they all took on board what you had to say.'

I allowed myself a moment of pride. She was right. I knew they'd listened, and it felt so good to be helping people again. 'I think I've gained just as much from them today,' I replied. 'I was worried they wouldn't be able to understand me and might lose interest, but quite the opposite. They've given me a real confidence boost.'

Mrs Armstrong and I made our way back to reception and I was signed out. We shook hands and agreed I would come back again in a couple of years to speak to the next batch of unruly teens.

I heaved myself into the car, slung my crutches into the passenger footwell and clicked on my seatbelt. All was quiet, everyone was back in class and the playground was empty.

I turned the engine on, reversed out of my parking space, and floated home on cloud nine.

21

•

A Dark Secret

I THINK AT THIS point I should tell you what happened to me when I was fourteen. But before I do, I want you to know that I'm not revealing it because I want sympathy.

I'm doing it because writing this book has made me reflect on many aspects of my life, and I'm beginning to wonder if the coping strategies I used to get me through that incident might have influenced the way I dealt with the aftermath of the crash.

During the Christmas break of 1987, I was on holiday in Morocco with mum, dad and my brother. The weather was amazing – baking sunshine, in complete contrast to the biting sleet we'd left behind in West Yorkshire.

Our hotel wasn't five-star luxury, but it was far from shabby, a typical family hotel with clean, bright rooms, some of which had views over the large swimming pool and sun deck area.

James and I were sharing, linked by a Jack and Jill door to mum and dad's. Separate, but still together.

We were there for ten days and on the first, James palled up with a bunch of lads his age, who then stuck together like glue. Being fourteen, I wanted nothing to do with twelve-year olds. Nor would I be seen dead sunbathing near my parents.

There weren't any girls my age, so on the second day, when a new bunch of guests checked in, I spied three good looking seventeen-year-old boys and thought things might be looking up. At least I would have something nice to view through my mirrored sunglasses. I was still quite shy at that age, typically thinking my boobs were too small, my bum was too big and my face too spotty.

When these Arabic Adonises confidently threw a soggy softball in my direction and asked, in broken English, if I'd like to play pool volleyball, I was thrilled and totally flattered.

They were so much fun and as the week progressed, I began to feel like we were a small pack. I was part of their group. When we weren't by the pool, we sometimes hung out in a small games room, where there was table tennis, snooker and a Space Invaders game.

Or we'd just go for a coke or ice cream at the café on site. One of the boys in particular paid me a little bit more attention than the others and I didn't mind at all because I'd developed a bit of a crush on him. He was cute. Even mum commented over dinner one night how handsome she thought he was.

We only spent a couple of afternoons apart, when mum and dad dragged James and I on trips to the medina and then a waterfall somewhere in the middle of nowhere.

On both occasions I couldn't wait to get back to the hotel complex and jump straight into the swimming pool.

Unbroken

At that age, who wants to be dragged round a baking street in Morocco? The boys taught me a few rude phrases in Arabic and I couldn't stop laughing when I got them to pronounce 'Eeh, bah gum'.

To other hotel residents, we just looked like typical teenagers abroad, having fun. They were charming and even had dad believing they were looking out for me.

On the penultimate day, we swapped addresses so we could write to each other when we got home and one of the guys asked a passing hotel resident to take a photograph of us all together. We were due to fly back on January 2 and there was a New Year's Eve party at the hotel before that.

Most of the guests were there, a real mixture of families, old and young, looking forward to seeing in the new year in style. I went with mum, dad and James and felt really grown up, being allowed to stay up until after midnight.

I knew the boys would be there too and was looking forward to dancing with them in the bar/disco area which had been decorated with streamers and balloons. The DJ played a mixture of European music. That year Fleetwood Mac's 'Everywhere' was really popular, as was Madonna's 'La Isla Bonita'. But when Ben E. King's 'Stand by Me' took the pace down a notch, I just rolled my eyes with the boys and moved back to the dancefloor perimeter.

We were all hot and sweaty, so they suggested moving further away, where it might be cooler. I'd have been happy enough just dipping my toes in the pool, but didn't think twice about following them down to a secluded garden area.

There was a row of benches just behind some raised planters, not visible from the hotel. It was much quieter because there was no other path running through the garden.

We plonked down and sat for a while, laughing at some of the parents' dancing techniques and the lame music we could just about make out in the distance. Then I felt the good looking one's hand on my knee and my head span round towards his. He was staring at me like he wanted to kiss me and, right then, I wanted to kiss him too.

But I didn't want to kiss him in front of his friends because, to me, it was a private moment. So I suggested that maybe they could head to the bar and we could join them in five minutes.

Things very suddenly turned nasty. The good looking one's face switched from smiley to menacing, like nothing I'd seen from him before and I felt very scared.

I pulled back slightly, questioning, wondering if he was joking, half expecting them all to burst out laughing, saying: 'Got you! Had you going there.' But instead, he pulled out a knife and held it to my throat.

The shock of it silenced me. I didn't know what to do. I was hoping they were still playing some kind of game and he'd toss the knife away and warn me never to go to secluded areas with strange men. Like a lesson of some sort, because they were lovely guys and would never hurt me, surely?

I was wrong. While the other boys jeered, he reached a hand up my skirt and tugged down my knickers, while still holding the knife to my throat with the other hand.

I couldn't believe what was happening. I knew there was no way I could fight him off on my own, so drew breath to scream for help. One of the others put his hand over my mouth. Then all three of them took it in turns to rape me. I had never slept with a boy before.

At the time, I think some kind of survival instinct must have kicked in, as I just tried to pretend it wasn't happening. It was all I could do, out of sheer fright. I have no idea how long the whole ordeal lasted, or how long I was sat there for afterwards in pain. I can't remember them leaving or how I got back to the hotel, but know now that I was in a state of shock. The boys could have gone back to the party and pretended nothing had happened for all I know. I've blanked a lot of it out.

I can only assume that the reason I didn't tell mum and dad at the time was because I was scared the boys might kill me if I did. I must have done a hell of a good acting job because my parents never suspected a thing.

Now, of course, I can see that I was being groomed right from the very first moment they invited me to play volleyball. But did they know how far they were willing to take it, right back then? Was I just one in a line of girls they'd played this cruel trick on at the hotel?

Was this normal, seasonal fun for them? Who had brought them up to believe this was an acceptable way to treat a woman – a girl? Did they feel even an ounce of guilt for what they had put me through?

I never saw them again. The next day I deliberately got up much later, feigning tiredness from all the dancing the night before, then stuck by mum and dad in the afternoon. My parents just assumed I was sad because the boys had left, a typical love-struck teenager after a holiday romance.

Our flight was early the following morning, so I wasted a lot of time pretending to pack that day too. I couldn't wait to get back on the coach to the airport.

I was frightened to death, on autopilot, desperate to be home where I'd feel safe. But even when we landed back in England, I was still looking over my shoulder.

They had ruined any sense of who or what I thought *was* safe. I had been utterly hoodwinked and began looking at other boys and men in a different light, wondering if they were all capable of doing something so monstrous.

Deep down, I knew that wasn't true. I knew all men

weren't like that. But why had those boys chosen me? Did I look like I deserved or wanted it? Had I insinuated in any way that I was game for something so horrific, led them on? I didn't think so, but was beginning to doubt myself.

I tried to carry on as normal when we went back to school. When everyone was asking about each other's Christmas breaks I just said I'd had a great time and smiled when everyone said how tanned I looked.

That was the thing. I looked perfectly fine and healthy, but inside I was bruised mentally and physically, with a creeping panic about the possibility that I might be pregnant.

There was no way I could buy a test. Nobody would have believed me if I'd gone to Boots in Bingley and said I was purchasing it for a friend. So I had no choice but to wait what felt like an eternity for my next period. Eventually though, with a huge sense of relief, it arrived and, with it came a stronger determination to forget the whole incident.

Just a week later, however, something almost as traumatic happened. A letter arrived. I'd forgotten that I'd given them my address.

They knew where I lived, didn't they? I grabbed the envelope off the floor before anyone else could see it and hid it up my jumper, running to my bedroom.

My hands were shaking as I tore it open. Part of me was hoping it might be an apology, full of regret for what they'd done, but no. It contained the photograph of all of us taken by the pool before the incident and a detailed explanation of what they'd done to me.

They weren't remorseful, they were gloating.

I felt sick and just wanted to get rid of the letter, to burn the evidence. I tore it into smaller and smaller pieces, crying at their cruel reminder, humiliated at my own stupidity for believing they were nice people.

I gathered up all the pieces and stuffed them to the bottom of my wastepaper basket, then left for school.

When I got home, I tied up the bag with the rest of my rubbish and, when everybody else seemed busy, took it to the outside bin and buried it near the bottom. I couldn't wait for the dustmen to take it away.

As I now know, you can't keep things buried forever, particularly emotions, so it's probably no surprise that it all came bubbling to the surface in a biology lesson months later.

I don't know the specific trigger, but I just broke down in tears, seemingly out of the blue. The teacher came over and took me to the deputy head, so she could continue her lesson.

The deputy head was amazing. I was crying and crying but it was a relief to be able to tell somebody. She just sat there and listened. She wasn't all, 'there, there,' she was just lovely, and very pragmatic, talking about what we needed to do and ringing my mum to come and collect me.

Looking back, I can't even begin to imagine how mum must have felt hearing that information and I honestly can't remember what she said or how she was. I was just so pleased she was there and already felt better having got it out in the open.

After that, mum and I went home and she went into practical mode. We booked an appointment with the nurse to make sure I hadn't caught any STIs and found a counsellor, who I saw a few times. In some respects that was useful. The one good thing was when she asked me to write everything that had happened down, and how I felt about it.

In the end, though, I just didn't want to keep raking it over, couldn't see the point in doing so. I told mum I'd had enough, that I felt better, and she let me stop going.

Back at school, I told the girls I was hanging out with that it must have been hormones that made me cry in the biology lesson, and they didn't ask any more questions. They weren't great friends anyway and I was trying to distance myself from them. It was about a year or so later when I made the lovely friends I've got now, but even with them it's not something we discuss.

They know about it, but I've never brought it up since and neither have they. Nor have I discussed the subject with mum again. I'm sure if I wanted to I wouldn't be shut down but, frankly, I feel like I've put them through enough.

There's only one other person I've spoken about it with, and that was after she unwittingly told me about a similar situation she'd faced. I felt like I could share my story with her and think we both gained a bit of strength from each other, knowing we weren't alone. For the sake of her privacy, I'm not going to reveal her name, but if she's reading this she'll know how she helped me.

Neither of us can bear to hear the word 'rape' now though, particularly when it is used in the wrong context. It makes me really cross.

I never tried to prosecute. I was too young and couldn't have faced the repercussions of people knowing what had happened. I can't even remember the boys' names now and certainly didn't keep hold of their addresses after that night.

I haven't forgiven them, not one single bit, but feel I'd be wasting a lot of negative energy on trying to track them down and bring them to justice now. I'm done with courts.

I just hope that as they've grown up and perhaps had daughters of their own, they feel remorse for what they did.

During the course of putting this book together, that incident has come to the forefront of my mind again. This time though, rather than trying to stifle the truth about it and therefore my feelings, I want to get past it for good.

So that's another reason why after all this time I am

giving therapy another shot. If there is a link between that incident and my subsequent poor choice of boyfriends, I want to change it. I am not a doormat anymore and won't settle for second best ever again.

I know I'm not the only girl (or boy, for that matter) who has just tried to get on with life after rape, but perhaps in light of the #MeToo movement, more people will feel empowered to speak out.

Maybe I only feel capable of addressing it now because so much time has passed since the incident took place.

I do know one thing for definite, though.

It. Was. Not. My. Fault.

22

•

Driving Me Up the Wall

I REALLY FELT LIKE things were on the up in 2005. I'd walked a mile, spoken in front of hundreds of teenagers, and accepted that I wasn't going to be a paramedic again.

I was getting physically stronger and mentally more resilient and now wanted a bit more fun with my challenges. I needed to push myself harder and try more things that I'd never done before.

The following year, I thought I'd have a bash at climbing. I'd learned to walk again, so surely it couldn't get much harder than that, could it?

My main carer at the time was Liz, who knew of an indoor centre near Elland Road, where Leeds United play. Her husband is an LUFC fan and she'd spotted the venue after dropping him off at the stadium one day.

Liz wasn't in the slightest bit surprised I wanted to try climbing because she'd been with me for a long time already and knew what I was like. She was my carer for about fifteen years altogether and only really finished because it got to the point where I simply didn't need help anymore.

Liz had done such a good job over the years of enabling me to do everyday tasks like shopping, cooking and cleaning that she kind of promoted herself out of her position.

One of the things we bonded over was our love of a Canadian band called Nickelback. I could listen to their best-known song 'How You Remind Me' on loop.

Liz and I took full advantage of the fact that, as a disabled person, I not only get a front row position at gigs for the wheelchair access, but can also take a carer along for free.

We saw them twice together. I'd buy the tickets and drive us there and Liz paid for dinner beforehand.

We had such a laugh, usually about the fact that it looked like I'd gone to the concert with my mum, because Liz was in her sixties. We still meet up now and again for lunch and she always supports my various fundraisers.

Liz booked an initial appointment at the climbing centre for me, so I could give it a try. I could have joined in with one of their weekly sessions they call 'Hoist', for people with disabilities, but I don't like being lumped in with generic groups. I think it takes away your dignity and draws attention to how you're not like the rest of the population if you are part of a special gang.

Maybe more fool me. I could be missing out, but I have to be honest about the way I feel. I want to be surrounded by people who can walk, talk and do.

The same goes for boyfriends too, actually.

It probably sounds awful, but if I went out with a wheelchair user, I know we'd just draw more attention to ourselves – and not for the right reasons.

And on a practical level, if neither of us could walk

properly, how would we get the wheelchairs in the boot? Life is complicated enough without adding an extra layer of drama on top.

The guy who helped me on a one-to-one session at the climbing wall was Pete. He was fantastic and didn't treat me any differently to anybody else in the place.

First of all, I had to sign a waiver, just like anybody who uses the climbing centre, to confirm I was fit enough within my limits and didn't have any behavioural issues that might create a danger to myself or others. As if.

Then I had to hand my shoes in and put some proper climbing pumps on. They are just like trainers but a bit more pointy, with extra rubber around the edges for grip. I'd already come prepared in leggings, so didn't need a full costume change.

I walked with my sticks into the main area where Pete described the different walls and various safety issues. The floor looked like concrete, but felt springy underfoot. It's a special stuff called rubber crumb, which basically means that, if you fall, there is a decent amount of cushioning and it's non-slip.

I told him that the last time I'd been abseiling was on school camp when I was thirteen, but that my plan now was to re-learn the skill, then climb a mile to raise money for The Smart Risk Foundation.

He thought it was a brilliant idea and took me over to the ten-metre wall. We both looked up to the top of it and he said: 'Right, well, once you've had a few training sessions, you'll just have to go up and down this until you've clocked a mile.' I loved the fact that he was so on board.

Then we went to get a harness. The good thing is that it doesn't look much different to the kit an able-bodied person would use. It's called a Karver kite harness. If you've ever been paragliding on holiday, it's exactly like the thing you'd be strapped into before being dragged behind a speedboat.

Pete attached some rope and a carabiner or two and then explained how I was going to get myself to the top.

Liz's face was a picture. She was going nowhere near the climbing wall and took herself off for a coffee, where she could get a good view.

Pete used a two-to-one pulley system, whereby the main rope was looped around the clip at the top of the wall, attached to my harness, then further attached to Pete, so he could be the weight behind me if I needed extra leverage up, or could make sure I didn't crash down with a thump.

The 'holds' felt strange in my hands. They are shaped like stones but made of acrylic and secured to the wall for climbers to grab on to. They are in different colours too, the idea being that you can pick a route up the wall depending on ability. To be honest, I wasn't bothered about following a route – I just grabbed the ones nearest to me.

Climbing took quite a bit of getting used to because I was using a whole different set of muscle groups again.

A lot of emphasis is on hands and fingertips and being able to angle your ankles in such a way to keep as safe as possible. I've still got slight ataxia (a movement disorder that means parts of my body don't always do what I want them to). It's a lot better now than it used to be, but occasionally I'll have a wobble and drop something. I managed to spill a Pot Noodle over my thighs recently and it didn't half scold.

But that first session gave me a real taste for what I might achieve. It was exhausting but great fun and I felt a real sense of achievement.

As my session came to a close and I was unclipped, de-harnessed and re-shoed, I was certain that, with practise, I could climb a mile.

So just like with the walking, I thought I should seal the deal by setting a date and telling the media. *BBC Look North* put it in their planning diary and told me there was a possibility they might cover the story, depending on what other news was around. I prayed for a slow-news day.

Liz and I went to the climbing wall every week for a few months until I felt confident. By the time the big day came around, I'd managed to convince a few other friends to join me on the challenge – climbing alongside me for support.

My brother James was brilliant and went up and down that wall heaven knows how many times with me, but the person who impressed me the most was my friend, Bee.

She is as scared of heights as I am of water, so she really faced her demons to support me. She's more of a yoga girl than a thrill-seeker, preferring peace and quiet to activities which scare you stupid. But to help me, she'd tied back her blonde hair, put on some comfy shorts and got clipped onto a rope. Watching her determination over her nerves really gave me a boost and took my mind off the fact that my bum was numb and my arms felt like jelly.

Look North sent one of their reporters halfway up the wall to interview me. They asked how far I'd climbed, how I felt, why I was doing it. Then, in the middle of their next question about why I'd chosen The Smart Risk Foundation as a charity, I suddenly disappeared from view.

I'd lost concentration a bit, my hand slipped off one of the holds and I began coasting down the wall. Obviously, Pete was there on the other end of the pulley, so I didn't go crashing right to the bottom, but it looked hilarious when we watched it back.

I managed to raise two-and-a-half thousand pounds and climbed more than a mile, another target satisfyingly smashed. To celebrate, I got a tattoo. You might think after an accident like mine that the last thing I'd want would be to suffer unnecessary pain, but I've got a thing about tattoos.

My first was a dolphin I had done at seventeen, but now I'm having to resist the urge to get more. It's almost an addiction. I wouldn't go the full David Beckham or turn into that creepy lizard man with the split tongue (Erik Sprague), but I couldn't categorically say that I've had my last one.

My dolphin tattoo is particularly unique. It sits just below the belt line but, after the accident, they had to cut me open down there and put a piece of metal in to hold things together. Some of my bone grew over the metal and, twinned with the scarring and stretching, it now looks like my dolphin is sat on a rock, growling. But after the mile-high climb, I wanted another tattoo to mark what I'd done. Nothing too obvious like a rock face or a carabiner, just something subtle.

I always go to Steve at Think Ink in Shipley, because he's so artistic and creates great designs. When you walk into the shop it looks tiny as there's just a desk and a huge pile of albums with drawings in to choose from and adapt.

Steve's wife works with him. If she's not tattooing, she is usually at the desk to talk through any ideas. They are a great team and Steve has obviously honed his skills on her body because she looks like a wonderful painted lady.

After a lot of discussion, we came up with the idea of some vines on my foot, because they could signify growth (I'd come so far personally after the crash). Also, vines climb upwards, so could be a marker for my accomplishment. Once we'd settled on the specific design, Steve printed it off to use as an outline stencil for the real thing.

Tattoos on your feet are the most painful because there's hardly any flesh on them, but when Steve offered me the numbing gel I declined. I honestly think I've got a very high pain threshold because it wasn't too bad at all.

The actual studio is in a room upstairs, away from the shop window. The walls are covered in photographs of other people's tattoos and music is usually on in the background.

The location of the tattoo on your body dictates where you need to sit or lie down, so because I was having this one done on my foot, I just sat on their normal tattoo bed.

When I had a huge Pegasus done across my back years later, I had to straddle the chair backwards and lean over it.

Whatever position I'm in though, the preparation is always the same. Steve wears surgical gloves, all the needles are sterilised, and the inks are lined up with the colours needed for that specific design. Then the area of my skin is sterilised too and work begins.

I'm sure it's different with every customer, but Steve and I just end up nattering through the whole process.

If his wife isn't busy she usually joins in, so it feels a bit like a social occasion, a therapy session, putting the world to rights one tattoo at a time. Maybe that's why I don't feel the pain, I'm too busy chatting. But this time, after I'd finished telling them both about my most recent challenge, they said I should take some time out for myself and go on holiday, relax a bit. Steve said if he was in my position, he'd open a holiday brochure, close his eyes and wherever his finger landed, book a trip there.

He had a point. It had been a while since I'd felt the sun on my body and, actually, it would be good to have something else to look forward to.

I began to wonder where I could go. I needed to be realistic – third world countries were off-limits in terms of general accessibility, but I was fine with long haul flights.

I still wasn't at the stage where I felt confident enough to go abroad alone though, so I had a choice – take a carer or treat mum and dad. I took mum and dad to Antigua.

23

•

On Your Bike

GOING ON HOLIDAY with family or friends can be lovely because there's always someone to talk to and you've got back-up in case anything goes wrong.

Antigua was amazing with my parents, and the Hawaiian island of Maui superb with another of my carers where, honestly, I accidentally wheeled backwards down a ramp, right into Pierce Brosnan.

I'm still thrilled with my quick response: 'Ah, Mr Bond, you should have been expecting me.'

His PA was less impressed.

But I still had that niggling feeling of wanting to prove to myself that I could go anywhere in the world on my own and so decided to set myself a two-year goal.

I would plan one more charity challenge for the next year, then make a break for it and brave a solo holiday.

I also wanted to up the ante for my next fundraiser.

Walking, tick. Climbing, tick. Time to cycle 350 miles through France and Belgium for Help for Heroes. Well, it's not a proper test if it's easy, is it?

I was never massively into cycling, so there was no real muscle memory to fall back on, but I used to enjoy messing about on bikes as a child.

I once rode to Skipton from Bingley with my friends Fern and Vicky, when we were about fifteen. It's a twenty-six-mile round trip, but we completely misjudged how long it would take to get there and back and ended up catching the train home. In fact, Vicky's got a really funny picture of the three of us looking shattered, with me cramming a Cornish pasty into my mouth.

I chose the Help for Heroes charity because I think a lot of people underestimate what servicemen and women put on the line just to keep us safe. They join the forces knowing there's quite a reasonable chance they could be killed in combat, lose a limb or two or end up in a wheelchair. Yet they still do it.

Help for Heroes is basically there to mop up the physical and emotional aftermath of those affected by war when the government stops helping.

The charity looks at the whole picture – not just the person injured in service – but their family too. They assist with physical rehabilitation, getting back into the workplace and supporting people's mental wellbeing after such traumatic events. They estimate that seven people a day are medically discharged from the armed forces, so a lot of people need a significant amount of help.

I was particularly interested in the Post-Traumatic Stress Disorder (PTSD) side of things.

Although it's a well-recognised condition for those who have been in warzones, it has only relatively recently been accepted as a condition for civilians who have faced something harrowing in their lives. It is brilliantly explained on the website ptsduk.org as a 'memory filing error caused by a traumatic event.'

A catalogue of events, influences and experiences can trigger PTSD, ranging from serious accidents (yep) to rape (yep), bereavement, bullying, childhood neglect, traumatic birth... the list is huge.

Surprisingly, it doesn't necessarily mean that you have to have been through these events first-hand, it could be that you witnessed them, or were affected by them.

When you look at it like that, my mum and dad may have had some form of PTSD following my crash.

James openly admits that he suffered from it, but I've always maintained that I never had PTSD. I'm not trying to hide anything, it's just not something I've recognised in myself. No doubt if there IS something there, my fabulous new therapist will dig it out for me to address at some point, but I'm not convinced.

There was a lot of training involved for this latest trial. Obviously, I couldn't use a normal, two-wheeled, upright bicycle, so I had a recumbent bike – the sort you sit down in and pedal. It's very low to the ground, so it wasn't easy for other road users to see me, but my dad came up with a brilliant way of letting drivers know I was there. He attached two enormous flags on poles to the back of it. There was no missing me then, with those wafting about in the air.

To be extra safe though, Liz would often jump in her car and follow behind as reinforcement. It must have been so boring for her just driving along, but I really appreciated it.

I managed to rope in my swimming instructor friend, Gemma, from the gym, to do the challenge with me too.

It was great having a partner to work with because we

could urge each other on. Gemma hasn't got any disabilities (apart from being my friend), so used a normal bike.

We spent months cycling around my very hilly village of Eldwick and Gemma's equally challenging homeplace Wibsey, an elevated area of Bradford, in all weathers.

When sleet and snow prevailed, we used the cycle track at the Richard Dunn Sports Centre, in Odsal.

It took the best part of a year to get my fitness levels high enough to manage the challenge, but just the training itself was helping me enormously.

It gave me structure and focus and a lot of laughs. This time, there was no need to involve the press because I knew that Gemma wouldn't let me get out of it even if I wanted to. We were in it together and that was that.

When we were challenge-ready, Gemma and I drove down in my car to the Premier Inn, Portsmouth, for an evening of 'getting to know one another' with everybody else undertaking it. Then we drove to Dover the next day for the ferry to Calais.

I have to say, out of all the hotels I've stayed in since my accident, the Premier Inn wins hands down in terms of accessibility. They just seem to know what they are doing and have thought through the layout properly. Even the next morning at breakfast, I noticed there was plenty of space between the tables for my wheelchair, while the buffet was at exactly the right height for me to see what was on offer.

Gemma and I had such a giggle sharing a cabin on the overnight ferry. The motion of the boat coupled with my sense of balance made for some top comedy moments. I must have looked absolutely hammered trying to move along the corridor with my sticks, and using the cabin toilet was a whole other expedition.

As for the main challenge, there were about sixty of us

taking part in total and it was a real buzz when everybody was ready to set off.

Some were able-bodied, others not. There were standard bikes, recumbent bikes and a few were using hand-pedalled bikes due to having limited or no use of their legs.

Everybody had their own story of why they wanted to do it and it felt great to be surrounded by so many positive people, all doing the same thing as me. Spirits were high as we set off en masse.

We called at the war grounds of Ypres in Belgium and finished at Dunkirk, France, which altogether covered three hundred and fifty miles.

Occasionally, I had to get the back-up van to drive me a short distance to the next place, which was annoying, but I accepted it. You have to know your limits.

I really was bone weary and it was very hot. So hot that the following year Gemma still had a tan line from her cycling shorts, after not putting enough sunscreen on her thighs and burning them raw.

We stayed at different hotels every night along the way. Let's just say that they were nowhere near the Premier Inn standard in terms of being wheelchair friendly.

There was one where I couldn't even get in the shower or bath, so just had to wash with babywipes that night, which is the last thing you need after a full day of cycling.

That was poor management from the company who had arranged the expedition, because they must have known that of the sixty people taking part, there were only about that many useable limbs between us.

But that was about the only downside. I met some incredible people. Those who'd been in the armed forces had real can-do attitudes, considering all they'd been through.

I really admired them for doing something positive out

of a negative and it made me feel so lucky that I hadn't witnessed some of the horrors they had.

One guy I spoke to had seen his best friend killed in action, which must be close to the worst thing you could bear.

Thinking about their bravery and sacrifice got me though some of the tougher sections of the challenge.

When we finished a week later, the euphoria was immense. My knees were in agony, my ankles swollen and my pelvis was really playing up, but I just felt elated.

Gemma and I had made it to the finish line and who was there to meet us as a surprise? Mum and dad and their best friends, Glynnis and Stephen. It was great to see them coming into view, waving flags and cheering us on during that last push, making us feel so well supported.

All our training had paid off. We raised thousands for Help for Heroes and felt a huge sense of achievement. We all agreed that our ice-cold pink champagne that night tasted particularly sweet.

My celebratory tattoo for that milestone was an extension of the vines on my foot. Steve designed it to look like it is crawling higher up my leg. It's ace.

24

•

James Comes to Terms

WHILE I PLOUGHED ON with various escapades, the rest of my family's lives were slowly returning to normal.

Well, the new normal.

Dad had re-joined James back at Phoenix Fixings and mum did her bit for the family business by keeping the books straight and dealing with some of the more unusual customers. She seemed to attract them.

One guy asked if, as well as fixings for the construction industry, they supplied anything else. Mum said: 'Whatever you want, we'll supply it.' His next order involved orange flavour condoms. And she supplied them.

For James though, there was still a lot of inner turmoil.

Business was booming, but things between him and Brennan's mum were becoming strained.

James was spending a lot of what little spare time he had at the gym, punishing himself with harder and harder workouts to avoid any negative thoughts or memories. That endorphin high was becoming more elusive and the happy façade was faltering. He was driving his head so far into the sand, he was struggling to breathe.

Friends had begun to slip by the wayside because when they did ring to invite him to the pub he was either working, being a father or lifting weights. But there was one invitation he felt he really should accept.

One of the guys who'd raced past our car on the day of the accident was emigrating to Australia and having a leaving bash. My brother and this lad had been good pals in the past and so he didn't want him to leave the country with any bad feeling between them. Only thing was, *he* would also be there.

James reassured his old mate that in no way would he kick off and cause a scene. That would be the last thing he wanted to do at his big send off. But nor could he deny that he was nervous about coming face to face with my nemesis.

It wasn't the first time the pair of them had spoken since the crash. When I was in Chapel Allerton rehabilitation centre, my then fiancé rang James from jail.

James said that was one of the worst conversations he'd ever had, because neither of them had moved on in any way, shape or form. I could still barely speak and certainly wasn't mobile at that point, so it left my brother with a lot of mixed emotions. James felt guilty for taking the call, but it was clear that the culprit was genuinely distraught and needed an ear.

James could hear the prison noise in the background – shouting, the clanging of iron bars, echoes of arguments – as *he* kept repeating: 'I'm sorry, I'm sorry, I didn't mean to do it.' He was broken, James told me.

In a scary, unfamiliar place with no chance of escape? Er, hello? Well, I was in exactly the same situation. And *my* sentence was for life, not just six months.

But James listened, empathising with him to a degree. He knew it wouldn't have done any good to start having a go at him when he was practically on his knees.

Despite everything, he reasoned that he was just a normal bloke who had made a monumental mistake and wound up sharing a cell with a psychopath.

James said to stay strong and kept that conversation a secret for ages. One more thing buried. He certainly wasn't going to tell mum or dad and couldn't tell me if he'd wanted to, because I was in the throes of a pulmonary embolism at that point in time.

One thing that really bothered James, though, was an incident that happened not long after *he* got out of prison.

Some mates drove him over to James's house, where he had been acting like nothing had happened, all cheery and chatty. That really upset James, who said it was like a smack in the face because I was still in Chapel Allerton. But James didn't rise to it in the moment. He just took it all in, bottled it up and didn't mention it to a soul.

Come the leaving bash, the dust had settled somewhat, and James didn't want to cut off his nose to spite his face by missing the chance to say goodbye to his old pal properly.

The party was held in a nearby golf club and James arrived quite early on. He still had Brennan to consider, so didn't want to be home too late. He'd said hello to a few familiar faces as he made his way over to the L-shaped bar and, spotting the departee, ordered a couple of pints before sliding one over to him.

The future émigré was telling him all about his plans for Australia, where he was going to live, places he wanted to visit en-route, the people he was going to meet up with and the job he was going to do out there.

It all sounded exciting and a million miles away from

James's life of responsibility. But James had one ear on what his mate was saying and another listening out for *his* arrival, inwardly churning because he felt that in some way he was betraying his family by even agreeing to be there.

The room was beginning to fill up and, as this mate went off to greet one of his relatives, James looked across the bar and spotted *him*. He looked like he'd seen a ghost, but James thought it best to take the bull by the horns, so picked up his pint and wandered over.

It was very casual by all accounts. James just asked him how he was doing, what he was up to, that kind of thing. It was all very surface chat, but nonetheless the ice was broken.

The conversation didn't last long – there were a lot of people coming and going and James wanted to chat to other mates too. But at the end of the night they shook hands.

James didn't say, 'I forgive you,' but both knew that, after that, there'd never be an issue if they were in the same room again. In fact, James says it was quite cathartic being able to look him in the eye and extend his hand. He was sick of carrying the weight of worry about what might happen if they bumped into each other. They lived in neighbouring villages, so it was bound to happen at some point.

When James got home that night, he felt a little bit lighter. The seed had been planted in his brain that perhaps acceptance, if not forgiveness, could lead to some sense of calm in his life, and he wondered if maybe the best way to find that might be through counselling.

He'd already had therapy not long after my accident, but never really felt he got to the bottom of anything.

It was a long time after the leaving party, though, when James finally reached a point where he felt he had no option but to go full throttle with psychotherapy. And to this day, he says it's the best thing he ever did.

Unbroken

James admits now that there was a moment before starting therapy when he fleetingly considered taking his own life. He never got as far as actually planning anything, but just felt like he didn't want to be here anymore. He was exhausted from wondering which mask to wear for which social situation and had begun to lose sight of who he was.

Nor was it helped by the fact that he and Brennan's mum had finally decided to separate. He was all at sea, trying to power on with his head in a massive jumble.

Until, after a few years, a girl in the office caught his eye. Isobella and he had been colleagues for a while, then became friends and eventually partners.

Everybody in the office was relieved because it was clear that Isobella made James very happy and the domino effect was happy manager, happy team. Their relationship blossomed and Isobella eventually moved in and now has a fantastic relationship with Brennan too. They got married a few years ago and the wedding was lovely.

Much as Isobella loved James, she felt he still had some demons that needed exorcising and that the few flashpoints in their relationship were always based around stress levels that she wasn't prepared to let ruin what they had together.

After a bit of cajoling, it was Isobella who got James to the psychotherapist in the end. They went together initially, and James believes it not only saved their relationship but genuinely made him a much happier person.

Catherine, the therapist, said things to them both which really glued them together. It was as if the stars had aligned and he could see clearly for the first time.

By all accounts, the sessions were very emotional, but doors were opened in his mind he didn't realise had been shut, never mind padlocked. He learned ways of thinking and looking at things, to forgive others more readily, but most importantly, how to forgive himself. He learned to let himself have his own thoughts and opinions and not be afraid to voice them. The chip on his shoulder was shaken off and he began to enjoy social occasions with all and sundry, rather than worrying about what everyone might think of him.

But the thing that surprised him the most was when he suddenly found himself smiling, involuntarily. Like a typical bloke he said it felt 'proper weird' to let his guard down and do the open-feelings thing.

He really had stepped out of the wilderness.

James has forgiven my ex-fiancé for the accident, but not for the way he treated me afterwards. Otherwise, my brother has let go of the events of 31 August 1998 for good.

James just wishes mum and dad could find it within themselves to forgive *him* too. He'd love dad to stop carrying the hatred around and reckons they would both benefit from therapy themselves.

It's true, you can't make an omelette without cracking an egg. But my view is that everyone is different and we all cope with things in our own way.

There is no denying that counselling worked wonders for James – and I am more open to it now than I've ever been. But if mum and dad say that it's not for them, then it's not for them. We all have to respect that.

25
•
Travelling Solo

I WAS ITCHING TO prove to myself and others that having a disability did not mean having to curb my wanderlust.

The time had come for some solo globetrotting and, as far as I could see, if companies advertised their destinations as wheelchair-friendly that meant they were George-friendly too.

I approached each trip with optimism and, for the most part, enjoyed the experiences and met some smashing people. But somehow, trouble always seemed to seek me out.

I thought a cruise might be a gentle way to start, with them being pretty much self-contained. It would be a good idea to have no hills or cobbly streets to negotiate, go where I wouldn't have to worry about cooking and had plenty to see and do along the way. What could possibly go wrong?

The package deal included a flight to Barbados, where I would board the ship. That might sound flash, but I had no family relying on me financially, no kids to support through school and university, no extra meals to make or clothes to buy and only one holiday ticket to purchase.

I'm a firm believer in seeking out the positives and I honestly don't think anyone could blame me for what might appear, on the surface, to be quite the splurge.

The flight went quite well. I had plenty of leg space and wasn't seated next to a baby. The issues began when I boarded the boat.

Everybody else was shown the safety drill, which explained where the life vests were stowed, what to do if the sea got exceptionally choppy and how to call for help.

But I was taken straight into my room without being given any information about how I could try to save myself if needed and, to be honest, I was already at a disadvantage due to my inability to swim and fear of water.

I couldn't understand their decision. Did they think I wouldn't comprehend the complicated instructions? Maybe they thought I wasn't worth saving.

It wasn't a good start, especially as I'd specifically rung up the holiday company beforehand to check that the ship was equipped for wheelchair users.

They'd told me it was, but I soon found out that it was only suitable for those people who'd brought someone else along to push them. Even the simple act of getting in and out of my room became a major struggle because the ship doors were so heavy.

There were two disabled rooms on my corridor. They like to keep us wheelers in the same place. But unfortunately, the chap next door decided we should be best friends and wouldn't leave me alone.

Even if he'd had functioning legs, he was just too keen and simply not my type, so I quickly devised an avoidance plan. I noticed he was a late riser, which was great because that's the complete opposite to me. I made sure to be by the pool for 8.00am, and back by 1.00pm.

Then I spent the afternoons at the other end of the cruise liner on high alert, not too far away from the cinema, where I could quickly duck in if I spotted him. I ended up watching *Harry Potter* about eight times just to dodge his radar.

One day I thought I'd mix things up a bit and change where I was sitting. I was on holiday after all, so didn't think I should be constrained by an on-board stalker.

My wheelchair obviously makes me conspicuous though, so I knew I couldn't completely hide. Nonetheless, I found a sunbed, got all sorted with my sun cream and towel and closed my eyes.

After a very peaceful half hour, I sensed him hovering, or to be precise heard him wheeling towards me. I decided to pretend to be asleep, but that didn't stop him from pulling up and bellowing: 'Ahoy, there!'

Not wanting to appear rude, I opened my eyes and smiled. 'Hello,' I replied, hitching myself up a bit. But as I did, my bikini top clasp snapped open and my boobs fell out.

Nor was that the worst of it. I thought I had a runny nose – maybe from the sea air. But when I sat up, I realised it wasn't snot cascading from my nostrils, it was blood.

I was having a full-on nosebleed and must have looked like I was in a slasher movie. It was all very embarrassing, but on the upside, he didn't hang around and never bothered me again for the rest of the trip.

On cruises, if you're single, the crew encourage you to sit with a variety of different people at mealtimes. Share you around a bit in the hope you'll fall in love and repeat the holiday together the following year.

Come the last night, I found myself lumped in with a group of slightly older people and placed next to a man who looked like he'd rather be anywhere else on earth than a luxury cruise ship.

I tried my hardest to draw a bit of conversation out of him, all the standard questions like: 'Is this your first cruise?' No. 'Which stop-off have you enjoyed the most?' The first one. 'Will you cruise again next year?' Doubt it.

After the starter, I gave up and concentrated on looking out of the window. Normally, I would have been worrying that he couldn't understand me, but he could hear me well enough because he answered my questions.

I bolted my main course down and then excused myself, heading to the bar for a few gin nightcaps with a couple of friends I'd made earlier in the week.

After a slightly wobbly wheel back to my cabin, I then packed the last few bits into my suitcase and clambered into bed.

As I attempted to drift off I mused that, on the whole, it had been a reasonably successful venture. I'd enjoyed the sunshine, the scenery, the food and drink and even made a few holiday buddies. I was wondering where I could go next.

Sleep was fitful that night though because I knew I only had a few hours to get my head down. We were docking in Fort Lauderdale at 5.00am and I was due to be picked up from the ship and driven to the airport.

Even though it was an eye-wateringly early start, I was looking forward to a relaxing breakfast in terminal two and a browse around some of the shops. I also couldn't wait for my own bed again.

But just as sleep began to envelop me, the captain announced an emergency on the tannoy: 'Man overboard!'

I couldn't quite get my head around what I was hearing

in that half-slumbered state. It took a few minutes for me to realise that one of the passengers had either jumped, been pushed or fallen off the ship.

Rubbing sleep from my eyes, I calculated that out of everybody I'd met onboard, it was unlikely to be anyone I'd spoken to.

I just hoped and prayed that, while the rest of us were told to stay in our cabins, those searching for the person (the lifeguards, police, army and coastguards) would eventually find them alive.

After about an hour, the tannoy crackled into action again to inform us that a man had been rescued and was being cared for by on-board paramedics. Now that's a job I would have loved, being paid to cruise around the world and defibrillate the odd pensioner? Perfect.

There was no chance of me getting anymore sleep now I was wide awake, so I cut my losses and got ready to disembark.

On the way out, I collared a member of staff and asked who had been for an unexpected dip in the ocean. It was the man I'd been sat next to at dinner that night. I hope I hadn't been the one to send him overboard by not sticking around for dessert.

Due to all the kerfuffle, we docked late, which meant I had no time for a leisurely breakfast or retail therapy at the airport. They just dumped me at the self-check-in desk with my luggage and left me to it. Sometimes people just don't think.

How on earth was I going to haul my suitcase onto the scales and scan my ticket? Or get from there to the departure lounge in time? Luckily, one of the air hostesses could see my predicament and sorted out the logistics.

By the time I got buckled up on the plane, I needed the

loo. The cabin crew team had been quick to say: 'If you need anything at all, just ring the bell and we'll help.'

I didn't want to be a pain though, so decided to wait a while before buzzing. When I did, there was no response.

I waited a bit more, rang the bell, nothing. Fourth time, someone came, by which point I was literally bursting. I thought I was going to wet myself as she slowly walked me to the loo. She said: 'When you're done, just open the door and I'll take you back to your seat.'

I did what I had to do, opened the door and realised the crew member was nowhere to be seen. There was just one other lady waiting for the toilet, wondering why I wasn't budging. We didn't speak the same language, so when I jokingly gestured for her to sit on my knee, she nearly did.

When I eventually made it home, I collapsed in a heap on my bed. Travelling solo is a real learning curve.

For a start, it is physically demanding in that there are always new surfaces to traverse, tricky doors to manoeuvre and airports to navigate.

There are unforeseen hurdles such as the realisation that 'wheelchair-friendly' doesn't always live up to its title.

Mentally it's quite tiring too, because I am always having to think one step ahead of everybody else and I do still worry that people might not be able to understand me in an emergency.

But it's worth it. I felt really proud of myself that I'd survived my first holiday on my own – virtually unscathed. With my confidence growing, I began to consider other options.

One thing that had struck me on the cruise was the fact that there were so many couples on board. Granted, some of them looked past the stage of being interested in a regular knee-trembler, but for a long time after the accident, I just hadn't really entertained the idea of a proper relationship. I'd spent so much time and effort fixing and improving my body, that I hadn't given much thought to finding a partner.

I was still nowhere near the stage of wanting to settle down, but was ready to see what was out there.

26

•

On the Market

THE WHOLE DATING scene has moved on a lot since the late nineties, when most couples got together through chance meetings in pubs and clubs or through mutual friends.

It was a case of seeing someone fit, giving them the eye and going from there. But now there's actual 'dating' and finding each other online. It's a completely different ball game with a whole new set of rules.

In some ways, dating apps are perfect for people like me – because it's easy to look at profiles and match interests before even leaving the house. But the drawback is that you obviously have to put your own photograph on there.

That made me nervous.

I knew I didn't look bad, all things considered, but I didn't want to be 'not bad for a spaz.' I wanted to look good full stop.

I'd been keeping fit with my fundraising challenges yet

I was still pretty chunky, so I decided to lose some weight before signing up for the online onslaught.

I joined Slimming World. It seemed like the best option at the time because they have easy recipes to follow and I liked the fact that I could go every week to get weighed.

It gave me more of a reason to persevere. I really went for it and put my all into their regime, but unfortunately ended up losing too much weight.

I got down to just over seven stone, friends started worrying about me, and mum hated the fact that she could see my ribs on my back. It took a while for me to accept though, because I didn't feel like I looked as skeletal as I did.

The problem I found with Slimming World was that it was all-consuming (no pun intended). Once I got into their programme of what was good or bad to eat for weight loss, it became a bit addictive because the results were so good.

Foods are categorised as either 'free' or 'syn'.

'Free' foods are classed as low-calorie but filling, and include such as lean meat, fish, vegetables, fruit and even pasta and potatoes.

'Syns' are the high-calorie treats which don't really assuage hunger, like sweets or wine. You're encouraged to balance it all up to ensure your body is still getting all the nutrients it needs, but within your allowed calories.

It's good in that there is so much variety you often don't feel like you're on a diet, but I took it too far and, in the end, the group leader asked me to stop coming.

In fairness, Slimming World have a duty of care and if they sense you're getting too thin, they have a right to refuse entry. I just had to take stock for a while and start eating a few more buns again.

Because I'd lost all this weight though, my boobs became a bit saggy; they were like spaniels' ears. The last time

I'd been in a position for someone to fondle them, my buzzies were still young, perky and voluptuous. I wasn't prepared for nature to ruin me before I'd had chance to re-live my twenties and thirties.

I very briefly toyed with the idea of using a push-up bra, or going to one of the high-end lingerie shops where you're measured, lifted and separated from your money. But in the end, I did my research and decided to get a boob job.

Nobody could believe that I was considering another operation after all the general anaesthetics and invasive treatments I'd already endured.

Friends urged me not to go under the knife for something unnecessary. But what they didn't realise was that for me, it *was* necessary. It was another step towards rebuilding my life. I wasn't after a triple-G Barbie doll effect; I merely wanted my double Ds back.

I had my initial appointment at the Yorkshire Clinic in January 2015, on my own the first time. Although I was a bit nervous, I needn't have been because it was all very civilised.

There was a lot of chat about why I wanted the operation and then they outlined some 'very unlikely' scenarios where things may not go as planned.

For example, allergies to the anaesthetic or my body's reaction to a foreign object thrust under my nipple. I was a bit like, 'Yeah, yeah, show me the samples, where do I sign?' I'd made up my mind.

Next, they put me in a vest thing with a bra on top and filled it with different sized silicone implants to get an idea of how I might look with other boobs.

As well as size, I had to choose from their shape options too – round or teardrop. Then I had to decide if I wanted my new boobies to be placed under or over the muscle.

The choices!

Over-the-muscle boobs are the ones that look fake, the type porn stars carry around. I opted to go for under, because I wanted them to look natural and match the rest of my body.

My operation was booked in for June and that gave me plenty of time to work on toning the rest of my body in preparation. Because I was already going to a personal trainer at the gym, I just asked him if we could ramp up the sessions a bit.

In fact, I still go to the gym three or four times a week for cardio on the treadmill, pull ups on the cable machine, tucks, obliques and lunges, plus a bit of floor work and stretching. I've got to keep my body as mobile as I can because, in all seriousness, I'm highly likely to get arthritis much sooner than most people. With my amount of broken bones, unfortunately, it's inevitable.

After six months of focussed working out, I was in tip-top shape and ready for my operation. It was strange because all the other procedures I've had were either in an emergency or in amongst my primary recovery; so it felt unusual being wheeled into theatre while perfectly well.

I didn't feel too great when I was brought around after the operation mind, but it was an absolute breeze in comparison to anything in 1998.

I was now officially the proud owner of two DDs again and, by the autumn, once everything had healed and I was signed off, it was mission accomplished and I was ready to give online dating a proper whirl.

Mum and dad still can't understand why my generation don't just keep it simple and hope to bump into someone they fancied, but they'd been lucky.

They met when mum was at teaching college in Kirkby. She had made friends with another trainee teacher called Jen, who she lived with in the refurbished old Nissan huts in the slum clearance area of Liverpool. One weekend, Jen invited mum back home, where she met Jen's cousin, Bill – my dad.

Dad eventually proposed to mum on Southport seashore. It was all very romantic, until dad tried to reverse the car out of the sand and got stuck. Luckily, their wedding at a Catholic church in Newcastle-under-Lyme went without a hitch, but the honeymoon got off to a shaky start due to dad turning up at the wrong hotel in Oxford; there were two with the same name.

It's a good job mum's got a sense of humour otherwise I don't think they'd have made it to their first anniversary, never mind their fiftieth.

In terms of my ideal guy, he has to be someone I just click with and, from experience, it would be easier if my parents liked him. Looks aren't the be all and end all, but he must have friendly eyes and a nice smile. It's the personality more than anything.

I know I said I wouldn't date anyone in a wheelchair, but that's mainly for practical reasons, so I wouldn't rule out someone with a disability if he could get around independently.

It would be lovely to have a partner who'd come home to me at the end of the day and we could have a laugh.

I'd even like cooking for someone else (a bit). Just a normal relationship, really. I never had that with *him* and I suspect that even if the crash hadn't happened, our marriage would have been far from a dream scenario.

I set myself up on one of the dating apps called Plenty of Fish. Their website says: 'We have thousands of singles on our site looking for someone like you. There's a high chance you will be matched with someone you like.'

Then it tells you their simple rules: 'If you see someone you know, do not publicise it. Do not spread rumours.

Respect our members. Do not date more than one person at a time.'

It wasn't long before I spotted someone I thought might have potential. We began to message a bit and then arranged to meet at a local pub the following week for dinner.

I was feeling positive, then a day or so before our date, his texts began getting more and more dull: Just cut the grass. Just had a shower. Just watching telly.

But since I'd already agreed to go for a meal with him, I thought I really should follow through with the plan. I didn't want to let him down. When I arrived at the pub and saw him, I knew immediately that he wasn't the guy for me. His photo was much better than the reality.

He looked about ten years older and a foot shorter for a start, but I couldn't back out now. He actually, honestly, talked me through the cooking instructions for a lamb's heart.

Then he proceeded to divulge the best way to catch, skin and cook a squirrel. I was beginning to wonder if he might be a serial killer.

I caught the eye of the waitress and silently pleaded 'help'. She twigged things weren't heading in a romantic direction and threw me a sympathetic glance.

She and I both knew there was no chance I'd be sharing a gooey desert with this guy, and a liqueur was most definitely out of the question. We'd met at seven o'clock and by eight I was wondering what would be worse, another hour with him or going squirrel hunting.

I let him enthuse about hearts and rodents for a bit longer and eventually told him I had to go at half past nine because I was busy in the morning.

The date had been precisely two hours and thirty-three minutes too long. But even when I was ready to go, my exit seemed to take forever because I still needed to gather up my crutches and wait for him to open the door. It was excruciating. (That's another annoying thing about not being able to move fast – you can't storm out and slam the door if you need someone to open it for you in the first place.)

He clearly didn't get the same vibes as me though because, when I arrived home, he texted to say he'd really enjoyed spending time with me, thought I was an amazing woman and suggested meeting up again.

Bless him. It was sweet and coming from the right place, and let's face it, who doesn't want to be wanted? But there was no point giving him false hope, so I sent one back saying: 'Thank you, you're lovely too, but I think we're two very different people. So good luck.'

He sent one back saying: 'How are we different?'

I said: 'Well, I'm not going to go into that, just know we are.'

And then I got another from him saying: 'Going to bed now.' But at least we'd actually got to the point of meeting.

I've had a few quite upsetting situations.

One was with a guy I'd been messaging for a few days before arranging to have a phone call. I'd warned him about my voice but, after an initial 'hello', he just hung up.

Another I started talking to proceeded to tell me I was weird. Charming. I try not to let it bother me. It's their loss.

When I took up pole fitness shortly afterwards, one man sent a message: 'You can spin round my pole anytime.'

Deleted.

27

•

Lure of the Pole

HOW I GOT INTO pole dancing was completely bizarre. It was after a dream, which I can still remember vividly.

I dreamt I was in a pub with all my friends and we were sat around a table drinking wine and talking loudly to each other over the pumping music.

Then the next thing, I was walking with them, unaided, to the dancefloor to watch a gorgeous woman with long black hair swooping around a pole.

As the disco lights dappled her body, she flung herself upside down, one leg looped around the top of the pole, the other outstretched, and slid down, staring right at me with a massive grin on her face.

In my dream, I knew I wanted to copy that woman and turned to my friends and said: 'I'm going to do that.'

They all looked at me so patronisingly as if to say 'Aw, bless her', but I was desperate to show them. So, I walked over to the pole (this is still in the dream by the way), hooked my leg around it and span. I could sense the wind on my skin as I twirled, feeling strong, free and happy.

When I woke up, I just lay there trying to recapture the memory. I hated the part where people treated me like an invalid, but there was something about the way the pole dancer had looked at me that really made me want to try it.

Once the seed was planted in my brain, that was it. I had the bit between my teeth. I got up and began my search for a pole dancing instructor stupid enough to take me on.

I scoured the internet, stumbling across all kinds of courses – some more savoury than others. There were quite a few specific adverts for gentlemen's clubs, where pole dancing and more were on offer.

That wasn't what I was after. I was doing this for myself. I'd been looking for a new physical challenge and this seemed perfect. It was fun, sociable and, frankly, just a bit crackers. It couldn't be more me.

But after a lot of browsing and clicking, I couldn't find anywhere in my area that didn't feel a bit seedy.

At the gym later that day, I told my personal trainer, Rob, about my plight. He said he knew someone who might fit the bill, a girl called Hayley, who ran Unique Pole Fitness, just outside Bradford. He urged me to email her and that's how it started. I told her all about my physical limitations, but she wasn't fazed at all.

In fact, Hayley was as game as me to give it a go and, five years later, I'm just a few sessions shy of achieving a 'Reverse Sunwheel'. Google it. I think you'll be impressed.

Most people don't realise that there are two categories of pole: pole fitness and pole dancing. That was the first thing I learned.

The second is that both are a lot harder than they look,

involving an inordinate amount of strength and endurance. Surprisingly, pole dancers don't do the same level of tricks and contortions, and pole fitness is much more tightly regulated.

Although they are similar, I opted for pole fitness because I liked the criteria. There's a lot of core training involved, which is fantastic for me anyway.

With Hayley, we also do a lot of biceps, lifting and conditioning. Although it's not dance-based, we do work on some routines, which I absolutely love.

Initially, I enrolled for a six-week beginners' course. Walking through the door on my crutches for that first class was another real moment for me.

I'd driven myself to the venue without a minute's thought and entered the room with enough confidence to be able to introduce myself without too much fear of people laughing at my voice. I was the only disabled person there but, at that moment, I felt more able than I had done since 1998.

The rest of the class were agog. They couldn't believe someone like me wanted to do pole fitness. I guess they just assumed wheelchair basketball or Paralympic curling would have been more appropriate. But once all the introductions were over and they knew I wasn't lost on my way to bowling-with-crutches they were very supportive.

I was starting from scratch, just like the others, so at least we had that in common. Like me, they'd all just fancied trying something new.

Hayley began with a warm-up; lots of stretching and limbering, which I joined in with as much as I could.

I was obviously no stranger to exercise, but I had to do things in my own way. Looking around the mirrored studio at the other girls I noticed that I was quite a bit fitter than some of them. A few were out of breath with simple sit-ups and twists. We were a mixed bunch to put it mildly.

Hayley demonstrated the first basic hand grips we needed to learn in order to get ourselves on to the pole.

Everybody had a go at doing it in turn, but when it came to me, I needed a bit more assistance. I could grip and move myself into the right area, but my upper body strength wasn't good at all.

Although the rest of the group were patient and encouraging, at the end of it, I felt like I was slowing everyone down. I didn't think it was fair that they had to hang around for me when they'd all paid the same money. It also put extra pressure on me, which I knew would mean I wouldn't perform as well as I could. It was a bit disheartening.

I went to one more class after that and then had a word with Hayley. We decided that going forward, I would benefit much more from one-to-one tuition.

I was obviously welcome to go to the rest of the other sessions but, to make proper progress, I had to admit that it would be better if I had Hayley's full attention and physical support. Since then, it has been fantastic.

One of the great things about Hayley is that she makes me believe I can do it. Mastering the physical aspects of pole fitness, Hayley believes, is mind over matter.

Whenever I'm struggling, she helps me engage mentally so I can visualise the next move. I know this sounds a bit new-age-hippy, but she's got a jar in her studio called a 'happiness jar', where you write down something you want to achieve that will make you happy, then work towards that goal.

It's all about positivity, which feeds into exactly what I'm about. I refuse to wallow and will always say 'yes', then worry about 'how' later.

Hayley and I began each session with a walking warm-up. I'd hold onto Hayley's arm and we'd walk from the front to the back of the room a few times.

But as we got used to each other and I became more supple, my grip loosened and eventually we reached the stage where I tried to let go a little.

It helped us build up trust with each other and now if Hayley asks me to try a new move I do it without question, because I know she knows my limits and wants me to be as good as I can be.

She claims I've helped her to be a more positive person too. I'm not sure how I've managed that, but I'll take the compliment.

The whole process has been a real learning curve. I hadn't realised, for example, that there are different types of poles for different forms of pole fitness: static and spinning.

They pretty much do what it says on the tin. Think of a static pole like a firefighter's. The spinning one looks the same as that but has an outer casing, which means you need much less momentum to fling yourself around.

The spinning pole was definitely the one for me. The only thing is, once you get going, it can be harder to stop.

After a few months with Hayley, I'd really got the bug. Her classes became the highlight of my week and I found I just couldn't wait to try each new move.

It wasn't just the fitness I was enjoying, but the freedom I experienced when I was out of my chair and not using crutches.

Hayley was obviously very busy and there were only so many sessions I could attend to use the equipment, so I decided to convert my spare room/office into my very own pole studio. Why spend time at a computer when you could be spinning through the air instead?

Typically, I went all-out. As well as a pole slap bang in the middle, I've got three sparkly walls and a fourth covered in eight-foot mirrors.

I also had a gym floor fitted to ensure a soft landing when (not if) I fall. It looks brilliant. You can imagine what it's like when I have people over for a few drinks, suddenly everyone thinks they are a Goddess and wants a spin, but it never takes them long to figure out that there's slightly more to it than flailing around, grinding your crotch.

Still, it's fun to see them try and fantastic that I'm better at something physical than an able-bodied person. I could genuinely beat them in a competition.

If I did want to start entering competitions properly though, my options are very limited. Obviously, I couldn't get into regular classifications because it wouldn't be a level playing field.

Even the disability groups (which I just hate the name of), have so many variations; for example, you could be up against someone partially sighted, but the rest of their body would be perfect.

I'd be at a major disadvantage before I even broke out the lycra and think that would be quite soul-destroying, so I'm just continuing to do it for fun.

Pole fitness is now a provisionally recognised sport in the UK by the Global Association of International Sports Federation. That's thanks to eleven years' hard campaigning by a fantastic woman called Katie Coates, the founder of the International Pole Sports Federation.

Provisionally means it's got something called 'observer status' – that they are going to keep an eye on the it, to see if really is a sport. Honestly.

Also in this 'observer' bracket are baseball, karate and surfing. How much sportier does a sport have to be?

Unbroken

I've heard a rumour that there's a possibility of pole fitness being included in the Olympics at some point in the future, although I'm not fussed about working towards that!

But I'd love to be part of a production. I heard a song recently that brought me to tears; it's called 'This Is Me' from the film *The Greatest Showman*. It's amazing.

When I played it to Hayley, she said: 'That's your routine song.' So I'm going to do it, just for the hell of it, even if I only perform it to the pole class.

There's a certain drum beat in the tune and when it drops, I'm going to drop down the pole dramatically.

Well, that's the plan.

It might take a couple of years, but I'm going to do it if it kills me. It's a pole goal and it's in the happiness jar now, so there's no going back.

The rest of the pole dancers who Hayley teaches are a lovely bunch. They often ask me out socially, but I'm just no good on a pub crawl, so usually leave them to it.

When on crutches, I can't drink. Well I could, but I'd probably break my neck again and it's not worth the gamble.

Nothing would make me risk the enjoyment I get from pole fitness now. It's the one time when I can express how I feel physically. When I put my crutches down and get on the pole all my worries seem to disappear.

It is in complete contrast to how I feel about getting around with sticks on a day-to-day basis. I must always be mentally one step ahead of everyone else.

I can't just get myself up a flight of stairs, I need to assess where my next crutch will go and check the handrail is sturdy enough, in case I lose my balance.

I'm also acutely aware of the surface of the ground. In the autumn I'm vigilant for wet leaves. In the winter, I have to keep an eye out for black ice. And at any time of year I'm paranoid about loose pavements, random bits of litter or other people gawping at their mobiles instead of watching where they are going.

Any one of those scenarios could render me out of action again. When I feel like I'm missing out on pub crawls, I just remind myself to balance up the odds and enjoy not having a hangover the next day.

Once I'd mastered some decent moves on the pole, I went along to a photoshoot which Hayley had arranged for her students. You can see the results on the cover of this book.

Her mum had a pub in south Bradford, and she'd let us use the function room upstairs for a studio. A pole and backdrop had been set up and we all booked ourselves in for a time slot with the make-up artist and photographer.

A guy called Shane did our make-up and he was a scream. He had a big box with absolutely everything in it anyone would need to look good... every colour of the palette imaginable, with any number of brushes, sponges and applicators. He asked what sort of look I was going for, so I showed him my outfit. After his eyes went back into their sockets, he told me to leave it with him.

He spent a lot of time perfecting my look, which I really appreciated. It felt like he was caking it on, but it needed to be dramatic to work visually with the lights and camera.

I had false lashes on too and he'd really brought out the red highlights in my hair, which I'd had done especially.

I'd also taken the precaution of nipping in to see Suzanne at Mirror Mirror earlier in the week, so I had no worries about unsightly face-fluff being caught in the backlight.

Once my make-up was complete, I went to the toilets to change into a black leather basque, lacy knickers and a masquerade eye mask with feathers.

Unbroken

When I emerged on crutches, Simon the photographer had to pick his jaw up off the floor. He couldn't believe the transformation from a girl with poles in jogger bottoms to hot as hell pole dancer. I have to say, I loved his reaction. It really was a thrill.

Hayley and one of the other girls from the pole class helped me get into position for the first picture, the lighting was adjusted and Simon began snapping away. I felt like I was on a film set, hearing the camera click as I span around.

I did various poses, but when I got into one called plank, he said he honestly had never seen anyone manage to hold the position so straight for so long. To say I was chuffed would be a huge understatement.

It was almost eight weeks until we got to see the photographs because Simon wanted to make sure everybody received them at the same time.

I felt sure they would look good, but when I turned the page to see mine, I started crying. I was completely taken aback by how able I looked.

Flicking through everybody else's shots there was absolutely no way on earth you'd think I was any different to them. It really was like my dream had come true.

When I uploaded them to Facebook my comments page went into meltdown. There was so much positivity from my friends and family that it was a bit overwhelming.

Hayley says I'm an inspiration to the others in the class now and often shows new starters the contrast of my photographs from just after the crash and my pole pictures.

I can't believe now that twenty years prior, when I was in Abbey Gisburn rehab centre learning to walk again, I'd wished my legs had been amputated at the knee.

I'd been convinced that it would have been easier for me to move around with prosthetics instead or, even better, blades, like you see on paralympic runners. But how would I manage pole fitness like that?

Any dance routine music would be drowned out by the sound of carbon fibre clanging against my pole.

28

•

Accessibility

ONE OTHER OBVIOUS drawback to replacing fifty per cent of my legs with prosthetics would have been the limited space for tattoos.

Knowing me though, I'd have sought out some of the amazing artists who specialise in designs for false limbs.

Nobody needs to have a dull, flesh-coloured prosthesis now if they don't want. Some people have whole cupboards full of different styles and artwork to match their clothes or mood. But as I've still got two full legs attached to a complete body, I've made the most of them with various more visits to Steve at Think Ink.

Over the years I've had roses done on the right side of my trunk (to match the vines on my leg), some butterflies on my other leg and a Pegasus on my back. But after the success of my photoshoot, I wanted one more biggie to mark the momentous occasion, so I enlisted the help of Hayley to choose an image with me. With Steve's guidance and input, we settled on a pole dancer design for the whole of the left side of my torso.

It's a woman in the 'Scorpio' position; upside down with one leg looped around the pole and the other sticking out to the side, both arms outstretched.

It's almost identical to the image of the woman in my dream and looks awesome. I was keen to show it off and thought what better way than in a bikini on another solo holiday mission.

I'd learned lessons from the cruise, so did my research thoroughly. I made calls to the travel company to ensure that the location and hotel I was after were fully accessible for unaccompanied wheelchair users.

She told me everything was in place for me to have a great holiday in the Bahamas. I was really, really looking forward to it. But before I could jet off, I needed to buy a few holiday essentials. I picked a quiet time to drive myself to the Trafford Centre in Manchester.

I like to shop there because its inside, flat and easy to park. But I face the same issue wherever I shop, that of getting my chair out of the car boot while still needing two hands on my crutches.

I parked and pressed the button for the boot to open, made my way to the back of the car and perched my bum on the lip of the bumper, thinking I could drag the chair out on its side. But when I reached over to haul it out, I lost my balance and found myself flat on my back on the tarmac, crutches splayed out.

I was livid.

I reached for one crutch, then using the tip of it, dragged the other one nearer to me and scrambled back up to try again.

Unbroken

This time, I managed to stay upright until just after the chair left the boot, but it was too heavy and took me down with it and for the second time in five minutes I found myself all akimbo on the ground, frustrated, wondering if all this was worth it for a bit of beachwear.

I knew I was going to need help, so swallowed my pride and flagged down a couple who'd just pulled in opposite me.

They had a bit of a shock initially because, when I waved and shouted at them, a car had just driven past and they thought I'd been involved in a hit and run. They came charging over, but once I'd explained myself and they knew I wasn't injured, they were hugely relieved.

Between the three of us we got the chair upright, and then got me in it. I locked the car and thanked them and although I was grateful for their assistance, I was annoyed about needing help in the first place.

Nevertheless, I wasn't going to let it spoil my day, and at least they were kind, unlike a lady in my local Post Office who once rolled her eyes and tutted at me for taking up too much space in the shop.

I'd already decided that I wasn't going to bother trying on bikinis there because disabled fitting rooms are generally a faff. I knew my size and just wanted to see what they had, make a few purchases and return what didn't look right once I'd tried them on back at home.

My problem is paying. Retail counters are always quite high up, so the shop assistant can't always see me, and being heard is tricky over the usual shop music.

Also, when it comes to using a debit or credit card, the wire on the card machine is rarely long enough to stretch down for me to punch in my number.

Meanwhile, the queue behind me grows...

It was good to be able to just wheel around the shops at my own pace and I ended up buying much more than I planned.

Carrying shopping bags can be tricky too because you can balance one or two on your knee, but they slide off once you start moving around. That day, I ended up carrying a couple of them in my teeth, until someone in Selfridges spotted me and offered to take them back to my car.

They went one step further and helped me get my wheelchair back in the boot too, without a hint of condescension, which I was most grateful for.

Recently, a journalist friend of mine borrowed my spare wheelchair and the pair of us went back to the Trafford Centre. The idea was that she could get a feel for what it's like for someone like me on an everyday basis. We ended up having a real laugh and one thing I wasn't expecting was that it was good to have someone at the same height as me for the entire shop. Plus, she was an extra lap for all the bags.

Everyday challenges for me were seen through a new pair of eyes. She hadn't realised how important it is to wear rubber, fingerless gloves when you're wheeling around, both to stop blisters and for hygiene.

If the wheels are constantly being dragged along the floor, you can pick up all sorts. Chewing gum is one of the worst. I'm not even going to go into dog poo.

Then there are the looks people give you or the comments you overhear.

When we were in Zara, a man pointed to us and said to his wife: 'Oh look, it's Bill and Ben.' Nice.

Once she'd got the hang of using the wheelchair, I sent her off on her own. I suggested a few shops for her to try before meeting up again for a coffee.

I specifically chose stores on different levels, so she'd

have to use the lift. And places with a mixture of flooring – laminate and carpet – so she could get a sense of how something as innocuous looking as a rug can present a multitude of obstacles. I didn't want to make it easy.

I headed off on my usual route, then waited for her return. She was fuming at Gap because they had a sale on, but the clothes rails were placed so closely together that she couldn't wheel in between them to see what was on offer.

There was a comedy moment in River Island when she nearly got stuck in the lift and apparently the man in WH Smiths gave her a very odd side glance when she asked him to reach a walking book off the top shelf.

I suggested she order the coffees. I sat there inwardly chuckling as she twigged the counter was too high, then had to ask for the hot drinks to be carried to our table.

When she joined me, I found out that while browsing in Lakeland for an ice cube tray, she was stalked by security because they thought she was trying to sneak it into a bag on her lap. But this is all standard stuff for me.

To end our trip on a lighter note, I said: 'I dare you to pull me along.'

She was game. I leaned forward, grabbed the handrails on the back of her chair and she sped off with me clinging on for dear life. We looked like some kind of special needs train and didn't half get some raised eyebrows.

The next day she texted me to say that her arms were absolutely killing from all the wheeling. I wasn't surprised.

That's one of the reasons why it's so important for me to keep fit and strong, because if I stop exercising then my muscles get weaker and if I want to keep globe-trotting, I need to be as capable as possible.

When it came to the Bahamas, I was adamant that I wanted very little help.

My outward flight went without a hitch. However, the rest of the holiday had its challenges and unfortunately, I ended up fighting back tears on the first night.

I was jet-lagged and starving, so made my way to one of the resort restaurants, The Tower. The *maître d* greeted me with a smile and a bit of chit-chat, then took me to a table that was positioned right to the back of the room, where nobody could see me.

I was really hurt, but didn't say anything. I just smiled and let him position me at the table. As he did so, I noticed there were plenty of other places out front in the busier zones. I could even have had a window seat with a fantastic view.

If I hadn't been so hungry, I think I'd have just turned right back round again and left. But I persevered, chose the easiest thing from the menu, which I thought would be the quickest to prepare, and tried not to catch anyone's eye.

I wasn't in the mood to start making new friends and the last thing I wanted was sympathy. As soon as my food arrived, I bolted it down, paid quickly and left.

When I got back to my room, I let the tears come. It was probably being over-tired that tipped me over the edge.

I woke up feeling much brighter but when I rang mum as promised – 'Just let us know you arrived in one piece' – she was fuming when I told her. She insisted on me bringing it up with the hotel manager, but I didn't want to cause a fuss, especially at the start of my holiday.

But then I thought, if I don't say anything, it might happen to someone else in a similar situation. I had a word with the lady on reception, who was most apologetic, to the point where I got a free breakfast.

Seriously, why, in this century, would any restaurant, hotel, café, bar, wherever, think it's acceptable to put the disabled one in the corner at the back of the room?

Unbroken

Once that awkward scenario was dealt with, I just wanted to enjoy the rest of my holiday. As it was relatively easy to wheel along the promenade, I took myself off for a bit of people-watching.

Dotted along the front were various sandwich boards covered in photographs advertising excursions to swim with dolphins.

Ordinarily, with my aversion to water, I'd have given that trip a wide berth, but after the restaurant debacle I was damned if fear was going to prevent me from doing what I wanted.

I'd always fancied swimming with dolphins, so thought 'stuff it' and booked myself in for the following day.

The next morning, I got chatting to an American woman as we queued on the jetty, waiting for the boat.

We were happily discussing the possible temperature of the water, how likely it would be that we'd actually see any dolphins, whether we'd done this kind of thing before and so on, but when the instructors arrived and introduced themselves, the American woman pointed at me and said: 'She can't talk.'

Honestly, it was unbelievable. Maybe she was deaf or hadn't been listening, but to say I couldn't talk, that really was something else.

With that comment, she genuinely did render me speechless, but I couldn't be bothered arguing. I was too cross so thought, 'Right, I'll just let them think I really can't and we'll see how we get on.'

To be fair to the instructors, they were only acting on what they'd been told, but it didn't prevent the standard over-loud, over-slow way they said: 'We're going to put you in your wetsuit now, ok?'

I just gave them a thumbs-up and kept my gob shut.

It was a bit mean really. I should have said something, but I had to roll with it once I'd started.

Luckily, I'd had the foresight to tick the 'non swimmer' box on the payment form, so they didn't just chuck me overboard. But I was nervous about holding on to a fin and being dragged too far out and, by way of some ridiculous sign language, I made them understand that I just wanted to float in the water with double life vests on and let the dolphins swim around me.

I have to say, it was worth my initial panic. They are such playful creatures and always look like they're smiling.

At the end of the excursion, I had to stop myself from saying thank you in case I gave myself away so, instead, offered some kind of half-bow, which looked and felt ridiculous.

Even though I'd squared up to my demons by dipping into the sea, it wasn't nearly as scary as my taxi ride back to the airport at the end of the holiday.

I was already feeling anxious when my pre-booked driver was late, but my fear ramped up considerably when he finally did arrive – with just the one arm.

As well as the practicalities of hauling my luggage into the boot, there remained the burning issue of how on earth he was going to change gears, because my carriage was far from top of the range. It looked more like RV Olop on her final journey to the scrapyard.

I kept schtum. I could hardly call someone out for being disabled and, as far as I knew, the vehicle might provide a very smooth ride.

The driver was remarkably capable, adeptly crunching from first to fourth with no hint of a swerve, but my sphincter went into overdrive when his mobile rang.

Without missing a beat, he switched to steering with

his knees and reached for his phone, I thought I was going to die – again.

I wanted to shout: 'I'm only in a wheelchair because of someone else's terrible driving,' but dared not distract him further.

As if that wasn't enough, his car began making strange noises and billowing out smoke. Sensing something might be seriously wrong, he steered it to the side of the road, where we eventually juddered to a halt.

My stress levels were through the roof by this point. I was late, traumatised and absolutely boiling sat in a car with no air conditioning. He just smiled and rang for another cab to take me and my luggage the rest of the way.

Once more, instead of a transfer which was meant to include a mooch around The Sunglasses Hut and dinner in departures, I ended up being fast-tracked straight onto the plane, which had been told to wait for me. I was about as popular as a bucket full of rattlesnakes.

To add insult to injury, when we landed at Heathrow, they couldn't find my wheelchair. When the captain realised my situation, he sought me out and genuinely asked: 'Do you really need it?'

I looked at him in disbelief and said: 'Yeah, kind of.'

After a period of monumental faffing around, they eventually located it at a different terminal and put it on my connecting flight to Manchester.

But I spent most of that last flight wondering if they really had found my chair or were just fobbing me off.

It was only when I was finally reunited with my wheels, and thus independence, that I could relax. Lost luggage is one thing because you can buy new pants and claim on your insurance, but a lost wheelchair isn't an option as you are basically losing your legs.

I won't give up though. I'm going to keep travelling until I find a company that doesn't bend the truth about wheelchair accessibility.

There must be a business somewhere out there who understands that a drop-down ramp from the pool to the cocktail bar isn't the only concession needed.

They must grasp that only when they can honestly say that a person in a wheelchair could access everything as well as a person with functioning limbs, should it be advertised as 'wheelchair accessible.'

And while I'm on a rant, most people in a chair or with crutches do not have unlimited funds, so it would be nice if some of the lesser-starred establishments would follow suit too, so we could all have the chance of snapping up a last-minute bargain in Palma, instead of breaking the bank on a hotel boasting spa facilities that we can't even use.

That wasn't something which concerned me in 2020 though, because like everyone else with holiday plans that year, they were swiftly put on hold when Covid-19 hit the headlines.

Unwittingly, the virus afforded me plenty of unexpected time to think and plan, galvanising my mindset for the next stage of my journey.

29
•
Frightening Flashback

MY NEED FOR carers had long gone. Fate had intervened, sending my three-person, twenty-four-hour team to their beds with a nasty bout of flu towards the end of 2015.

I'd made a point of never asking friends to 'work' for me, and mum and dad were away, so I was left with the choice of either going it alone or facing the hassle of getting temps in. I bit the bullet.

To my surprise, I could do a lot more than I'd given myself credit for. I could make myself basic meals, get in and out of the shower (not exactly gracefully, but still) and, because I could already drive, was able to get places.

Obviously, I needed help to hoist the chair out of the boot, but I wasn't above asking random people for assistance with that. By then, internet shopping was a thing, so I set myself up with supermarket deliveries.

I'll admit, it was more time-consuming and tiring than

I'd imagined, but as a few days turned into a week, and then another, I began to get a kick out of how much progress I was making on my own.

I started setting myself little time-goals to smash, like how quickly I could get the laundry from the basket to the machine, and how fast I could empty the dishwasher without smashing anything.

One thing I did struggle with was blow-drying the back of my hair. My arms just don't want to go that way anymore, so I looked like Worzel Gummidge for a while.

I was beginning to appreciate having time in the house on my own. I'd never lived alone before, having gone straight to Stafford, where I lived with Helen and Mabel, then America as an au pair, and Liverpool with lodgers.

In between jobs I'd been back at mum and dad's and you know the rest. But when faced with my own company, I found I didn't even have time to be lonely because I had so much to do. I'd get to the end of each day and just flop into bed with a feeling of deep satisfaction.

Before I knew it, almost three weeks had passed, and I wanted to make some decisions about my future.

Suddenly the thought of having people around me 24/7 seemed stifling and unnecessary and once everyone had recovered, we came to an agreement. Liz would continue to help me on a part-time basis and the other two were happy to find work elsewhere. I think we were all relieved.

We had all just got too comfortable with the set up and without realising it, the situation had begun to disable rather an enable me.

The next four or five years went by in a blur of pole fitness, training at the gym and various fundraisers.

I was venturing further afield in terms of travel, having lowered my expectations a little and learned to read between the standard agency lines. Then, at the beginning of February 2020, I started getting tummy ache.

It wasn't bad at first, more like a dull feeling, a bit like period pains spreading to my lower back, which I initially managed with paracetamol. But then at one of my usual training sessions with Rob at the gym, I couldn't even start the warm-up due to the agony.

Assuming it was something muscular, we called it a day and I went home to rest. The weird thing was, it hadn't affected my appetite – I still enjoyed a meal that night and kept myself hydrated.

But the next morning after an early breakfast, the pain was back – and this time it was horrendous. I thought I needed the loo badly but, when I got there, it didn't ease.

I rang mum and she instructed me to go to bed and drink plenty of water. Her and dad came to check on me at about 11.00am but there'd been no let up, so they helped me to the lounge and put the fire on, making sure I still had plenty of fluids to hand.

By 3.00pm I wasn't improving, so rang 111. They said my doctor would call me within three hours. When I reported back to mum, she said: 'Do you think your coil could have moved?' so I rang back and an ambulance was dispatched immediately.

It turned out I had two kidney stones. One was ten millimetres long, the other three. To complicate matters more, when they tried to remove them, it was discovered that I have two urethras, which is why the largest kidney stone had remained undetected for so long – and I'd developed sepsis.

It was all hands on deck as the surgeons raced against time to flush me with as many antibiotics as they could.

There was no time to remove the stones, so they encased each one in a separate, temporary stent and put me into an induced coma on the Intensive Care Unit. I was under for four days and, yet again, my brother found himself on the receiving end of a phone call to get to Airedale Hospital as soon as he could.

It was a frightening flashback for the whole of my family as they were told to expect the worst. Mum took charge of my mobile phone and texted my various group chats to let friends know.

Scrolling back now I can see how close to death I was, and how immediately everyone responded with offers of help, messages of love, thoughts and even prayers.

The thing with sepsis is that it can take hold so quickly, restricting blood flow to limbs or vital organs, sometimes resulting in amputations.

Not only were they enormously worried about my chances of pulling through but, if I did, whether I would still have use of my arms and legs if the sepsis spread.

It was too much to contemplate. Without legs, I could still use my wheelchair, but without arms, I wouldn't be able to push myself along and would have to start all over again with a motorised chair. Pole fitness would have been out of the question.

All I can say is that I must have done something right in a previous life because, yet again, I was spared.

I'm not making light, it genuinely was touch and go for a while, but by day five, I was well enough to be transferred to a recovery ward with all my limbs intact.

On the tenth day, I was allowed home with strict instructions to take it easy; no pole, no exercise and definitely no pink champagne.

I had to keep taking the antibiotics and a date was set for mid-April, when I could return to have the kidney stones finally removed.

Unbroken

It felt great to be back in my own place again.

A week later, the bombshell of coronavirus hit and my operation was cancelled. I had to self-isolate for twelve weeks because of my vulnerability with the kidney stones.

Although I was miffed, I knew I had to listen to advice and was just grateful that I could manage on my own.

As the death toll rose and I watched the chaos unfolding, I knew for sure that I was staying put for as long as necessary. There was no way on earth I was going to drag my family through another ordeal.

I just did what everybody else in self-isolation did – not much. I read a lot, watched TV, Facetime-d friends, attempted a jigsaw and just hoped that those allowed outdoors were being sensible.

I thought of the staff at the care home where I used to work, looking after elderly people with inadequate personal protective equipment to keep them safe.

I imagined how frightening and desperately sad it must have been for patients dying alone, without a loved one holding their hand. The stress those people working in the emergency services were under must have been off the scale.

On Thursday nights, when we all clapped and banged our pots and pans for the NHS, I was often overwhelmed by it all, in floods of tears for the whole shocking mess of it.

It made me realise how fragile we are and how grateful we must be to those who put their own lives on the frontline to save ours.

And I wished so badly that I could have done my bit to help, that I was able to hold someone's hand in the back of an ambulance, reassuring them that they were safe now. I wondered how Graeme's harmonica was holding up.

It was a fraught time for everyone, not just for those who were ill or helping others, but for people whose businesses and jobs were in jeopardy too. Priorities changed, belts tightened and many of us were forced into taking stock of our lives again, suddenly having a lot of time to think.

I was lucky that my operation was rescheduled for May, when the NHS re-opened for non-emergency procedures.

I was nervous about going into a hospital environment in case Covid was waiting to pounce, but Airedale managed everything perfectly.

I had completely recovered from sepsis, so was only admitted for one night because I didn't need a general anesthetic. They could remove the kidney stones after an epidural.

Everything went according to plan. The stones were taken out and sent for analysis and the stents just needed to be gently coaxed out a few days later.

I assumed they meant that I'd nip to the doctor's surgery in my village to have the stents removed, but no.

There was no need for medical intervention, they said, it was just a case of pulling on a string that had been taped to my inner thigh and they would slide out. I was concerned about doing this on my own, so commandeered mum.

We decided that it would probably work best if I angled myself into some kind of leg-up position, so she could see underneath my crotch to coax the string.

Using the bed knob for balance, I stood up and placed one leg on the mattress and she crawled below.

We were both expecting something about an inch long to appear, perhaps tubular in shape, but instead, what emerged was almost a foot-long piece of wire.

It felt a bit strange coming out, but it didn't hurt. Mum got herself back into a standing position and held it up in front of me. We just looked at each other and burst out laughing.

Unbroken

I was so relieved to be pain-free and particularly pleased that I could tentatively start exercising at home again.

My spirits were lifting but, like everybody else, I had no idea that after a summer of looser Covid restrictions, the whole country would be put on a tighter leash before being plunged into a longer lockdown.

And this time, we couldn't rely on the sunshine to see us through. It felt like we were in this for the long haul.

When you've worked for the NHS, it becomes part of you. The need to help others is in your blood. And even though I hadn't been part of the paramedic team since before the accident, I felt there must be something I could do amid the pandemic.

I was realistic. I clearly wasn't going to be sprung back into action with the blue light brigade no matter how desperate they were. But I could take part in vaccine trials.

I'd seen on the news that people were needed, so did a bit of Google-ing and was directed to the Synexus site.

Having read up on what was required, I filled out an online form to express my interest and a few days later they rang to book me in for the following week.

I'd been hoping to take part in the trial at Bradford University because it's nearer, but they were full and Synexus Clinic in Manchester was the next on the map.

The vaccine they were working on was the Novavax. It's what's called a protein subunit vaccine, which is a different kind of vaccine technology used in the shots made by Pfizer and Moderna.

My friend Luke came with me because I had no idea what to expect. We had to drive past Strangeways prison to get there, but the one redeeming thing in that area was a McDonald's and because we'd given ourselves plenty of time before the appointment, we treated ourselves to a drive-thru sausage and egg McMuffin. It felt like a massive treat, what with restaurants having been closed for so long. You've got to get your kicks where you can in a pandemic.

The actual Synexus building is a pristine clinic with uber-efficient-looking staff in PPE, all very reassuring. I was glad to have re-fueled before arrival though, because my first appointment lasted three hours.

First, I was taken through to an office/surgery, where they explained the details of the trial and gave me a consent form to sign. It was quite detailed and they were very open about any possible side-effects.

The next thing they did was give me a Covid test to make sure I wasn't positive. It was a swab thing right at the back of your throat and then up your nose.

They watched me as I did it to make sure I knew what I was doing because they also gave me three tests to take home in case I developed any symptoms.

The test was negative.

Then I had to do a pregnancy test.

I said: 'I'm definitely not pregnant – it's healed up.' They didn't think that was as funny as I did but, obviously, that was negative too.

Then it was onto bloods, where they check for pretty much everything. And finally, after all that, I was ready to receive my first dose of Novavax.

'You might feel a small prick,' she said and, for once, I kept my mouth shut.

After a half-hour wait to ensure I hadn't had any adverse reactions, I was free to leave. At this point, I wasn't told whether I'd been given the real vaccine or the placebo.

For the second appointment, two weeks later, we were only there half an hour. I'd already done the Covid test at home, so literally had the jab, hung about for any side-effects and then left. I had no adverse effects whatsoever after either dose. Then, at the end of December, I was invited back for an antibody test, so at this point was beginning to suspect I had been given the real vaccine.

Christmas and New Year came and went without much of a fanfare. I just felt very lucky to be safe, well, and able to see my family over the festive period.

After all the standard seasonal indulgence, I was ready to start January with a fresh focus on my fitness, regaining some core strength and stamina in preparation for when pole fitness classes re-opened.

In March it was confirmed that I'd been given the real vaccine. Against the original Covid-19 strain in the UK, the Novavax vaccine is about 96 per cent effective.

Against the new variant that has been circling in the UK since the start of 2021, it's about 86 per cent effective.

But for someone who was given a less than one per cent chance of survival after a near-fatal car crash, those are the kind of odds I'm happy to roll with.

I'd had to stop the sessions with my psychotherapist, Catherine, when my kidneys flared up. We'd only managed one meeting. Then lockdown hit and I didn't feel Zoom sessions were the way forward for me. When I eventually rang for a second appointment, she was pleased to hear from me and agreed we had a lot to discuss.

I told her I'd be coming on my own this time and wanted to check there would be somebody around to help me up the steps.

She arranged for us to use a different space downstairs which was more accessible and better for social distancing, if that was still necessary.

I thanked her, hung up and breathed out.

I have no idea where my journey with Catherine is

going to take me and, to be honest, I'm a little concerned she might think I'm a fraud.

I'm not unhappy, that's the thing. In fact, I'm more grateful than anyone could ever know that I'm alive and well.

But I think I owe it to myself to try to look at some of the tangled weeds from my past and if possible, get rid of a few rotten roots.

Who knows, after a bit of talking to Catherine, Dead Day might take on a whole new meaning.

Nothing is impossible.

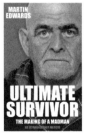

It was Booker Prize-winning author of *Schindler's Ark*, Thomas Keneally, who described Dave Hadfield as 'The Poet of Rugby League'. True enough, though the man who has also been called Bolton's answer to Bill Bryson has equally revelled in other subjects, like music and travel.

Lost in Spain is the result of the dying wish of Dave's oldest friend's wife, Barb, to have her ashes scattered along the route traced by Laurie Lee when he walked from Gloucestershire to the Med in the 1930s.

That original journey provided the material for *As I Walked Out One Midsummer Morning*, the book upon which, as well as *Cider with Rosie*, Lee's glittering reputation rests.

Lost in Spain is a story of friendship and late-flowering love that is by turns informative, poignant, elegiac and laugh-out-loud funny.

These days freed from the constraints of daily journalism, Hadfield has no plans to stop writing.

Of his ten books so far, five have been written since he was diagnosed with Parkinson's Disease in 2008.

DAVE HADFIELD

IN THE FOOTSTEPS OF LAURIE LEE

The Woman without a Number

The Woman Without a Number is the inspirational story of holocaust survivor Iby Knill, whose early childhood was spent in Czechoslovakia before her parents – alarmed at the persecution of Jews in Germany – smuggled her over to Hungary.

There, she was caught by the Security Police, imprisoned and tortured, not just for having Jewish connections, but for being in Hungary illegally and aiding the resistance movement. She was sent to the infamous Auschwitz-Birkenau camp.

In June 1944, Iby left Auschwitz-Birkenau by volunteering for labour at a hospital unit where she risked her life protecting the weak and helpless from the gas chambers before being freed by Allied Forces at Easter, 1945.

The woman without a number

IBY KNILL
An inspirational story of Holocaust survival

A sequel to The Woman Without a Number

The Woman with Nine Lives

The Barefoot Shepherdess

and Women of the Dales

By Yvette Huddleston & Walter Swan

The Barefoot Shepherdess and Women of the Dales celebrates the variety and versatility of determined women who have made a life for themselves 'far from the madding crowd'.

The Yorkshire Dales attracts tourists aplenty, but most visitors return to their towns and cities, renewed by the peace and quiet of the countryside, though unable to leave their modern, urban lifestyle for too long.

Women like Alison O'Neill, who owns her own flock of sheep and designs tweed clothing, demonstrate that you can live a life of independence and fulfilment in Britain's remotest regions. There are hardships to be endured but innumerable compensations when the Dales are on your doorstep.

Each chapter features women who made the choice to live and work collaboratively with the people and places of the Yorkshire landscape, whether they be farmers, artists, vets, publicans, entrepreneurs, artisans, academics, curators or vicars. And all have a passion for life.

Featuring personalities from the ITV series **The Dales**